Effective Commissioning in Health and Social Care

Effective Commissioning in Health and Social Care

RICHARD FIELD
AND JUDY OLIVER

Series Editor: Keith Brown

Los Angeles | London | New Delhi
Singapore | Washington DC

Learning Matters
An imprint of SAGE Publications Ltd
1 Oliver's Yard
55 City Road
London EC1Y 1SP

SAGE Publications Inc.
2455 Teller Road
Thousand Oaks, California 91320

SAGE Publications India Pvt Ltd
B 1/I 1 Mohan Cooperative Industrial Area
Mathura Road
New Delhi 110 044

SAGE Publications Asia-Pacific Pte Ltd
3 Church Street
#10–04 Samsung Hub
Singapore 049483

Editor: Luke Block
Development editor: Lauren Simpson
Production controller: Chris Marke
Project management: Swales & Willis Ltd,
Exeter, Devon
Marketing manager: Tamara Navaratnam
Cover design: Wendy Scott
Typeset by: C&M Digitals (P) Ltd, Chennai,
India
Printed and bound by Henry Ling Limited,
at the Dorset Press, Dorchester, DT1 1HD

Library of Congress Control Number:
2013940924

British Library Cataloguing in Publication
Data

A catalogue record for this book is available
from the British Library

MIX
Paper from
responsible sources
FSC
www.fsc.org **FSC® C013985**

ISBN 978-1-4462-8225-0
ISBN 978-1-4462-8226-7 (pbk)

Contents

List of figures

List of tables

Foreword

Commissioning is not a new concept to those of us who lead or work with health and social care organisations. However, our understanding of what works in terms of structures, relationships, systems and behaviours continues to evolve. Yet, for many people who work in organisations providing health and social care services, the word and the activities involved still remain a mystery.

In this text, the authors attempt to demystify commissioning, explore its benefits and describe associated key activities. They help us by unravelling its origins through to the current changes in the Health and Social Care Act 2012 to demonstrate that what is happening now is nothing new. Rather, it could perhaps be described as the continuation of a journey of discovery as the facets of commissioning have been tried and tested in different ways.

Looking to the future, the case is made for viewing commissioning on a whole-life basis to ensure a better balance between care and treatment, prevention and wellbeing. In order to realise the potential efficiencies and economies of such new developments as community budgets and community-based commissioning, many different types of collaboration will be required. In addition to technical commissioning skills, all those involved will need to be able to collaborate effectively between themselves, whether commissioners or providers, service users and patients, carers, families, neighbours and community organisations.

This book has been expertly produced by Richard Field and Judy Oliver. Their many years of experience of operating in health and social care contexts – from the board room, the council chamber to frontline services – are clear to see. To move forward in such financially constrained conditions is likely to require some 'disruption' to the current system. They contribute to this by constructively challenging the reader's traditional thinking and by posing questions of those that are strategically and operationally involved in commissioning.

It is my sincere belief that this text will be of benefit to all who work in this field and, ultimately, their clients and the wider community.

Professor Keith Brown
Series Editor
National Centre for Post Qualifying Social Work, Bournemouth University

About the authors

Richard Field is a qualified accountant, executive coach and a visiting fellow at Bournemouth University. Richard started his financial career with Essex and Suffolk County Councils before joining Anglia Ruskin University. Whilst at the university Richard helped public sector managers develop the skills they needed to flourish in contexts involving compulsory competitive and purchaser/provider operation – both forerunners of commissioning. Richard has worked for the Office for Public Management on a number of highly successful leadership programmes and at Bournemouth University he teaches strategic management and commissioning. Currently Richard is a freelance development specialist working with individual leaders, leadership teams, Clinical Commissioning Groups and Health and Wellbeing Boards. Richard facilitates leadership and organisational development, helping design frameworks and processes relating to commissioning. Richard is committed to helping organisations realise the significant opportunities offered by today's commissioning environment.

Judy Oliver is a qualified barrister, executive coach and facilitator specialising in strategic thinking, management of change and transition and the development of teams and partnerships. Judy started her career with BP, where she worked in a variety of roles, including industrial relations, legal, HR policy and management development of high-potential managers. After contributing to the development of the first public–private sector MBA with Warwick Business School, she transferred to local government, initially as Head of HR for Education at Kent County Council and later working directly for the deputy chief executive during the development of purchaser–provider arrangements. Since becoming self-employed in 1998, Judy has designed and delivered a wide range of bespoke leadership development programmes and workshops for leaders across all sectors but, particularly, for clinical leaders in the NHS. Clients include Clinical Commissioning Groups, Health and Wellbeing Boards, Primary Care Trusts and national organisations such as the General Medical Council and the Parliamentary and Health Service Ombudsman.

Chapter 1
Introduction

Welcome to this introductory text for professionals involved in, or responsible for, health and social care. The content will also be of potential value to managers operating elsewhere in organisations engaged in commissioning or providing public services.

Commissioning is not new. Its roots can be traced back to the 1979 Conservative administration which introduced a number of initiatives, including compulsory competitive tendering (CCT), purchaser/provider arrangements in social care, service level agreements, direct service organisations (DSOs) and GP fundholding. The Labour administration elected in 1997 abandoned DSOs and GP fundholding; however, not much later, they introduced other initiatives, such as Primary Care Groups and, later, World Class Commissioning in the NHS that encouraged or required a distinct commissioning role. The journey to commissioning continues with the coalition government and the Health and Social Care Act 2012. This act requires each GP practice to belong to a Clinical Commissioning Group (CCG) which are authorised to take over responsibility for commissioning budgets from Primary Care Trusts (PCTs). In recent years, many public sector organisations have started to work in more commercial ways with the private sector, and have adopted principles and practices typically associated with commissioning.

Alongside more commercial ways of working, there has been increased public service collaboration, including Local Strategic Partnerships, health and wellbeing partnerships, youth offending teams and community safety partnerships. Interest in collaboration has been stimulated by a heightened concern to tackle complex, cross-cutting problems, often referred to as wicked issues, to improve outcomes and reduce waste through end-to-end service redesign and achieve cost savings through shared support services.

Whilst much has been made of the potential impact of the Health and Social Care Act 2012 on the health service, local government in general, and social care in particular, will be significantly affected in two respects.

Firstly, there is a requirement to form Health and Wellbeing Boards that will include representatives from social care and other parts of local government as well as health. Health and Wellbeing Boards are responsible for producing both a Joint Strategic Needs Assessment (JSNA) and Joint Health and Wellbeing Strategy, as well as developing joint approaches to commissioning and providing.

The second aspect is the transfer of public health functions and staff into local authorities which will give health high visibility alongside social care and bring it within the direct influence of locally elected politicians.

The practice of commissioning is emerging and can be expected to develop further over the next five years and beyond. Structures, frameworks and processes introduced as a result of the Health and Social Care Act 2012 will need to evolve. What is already clear is that a wide range of stakeholders will need to develop technical competence in commissioning and the ability to lead in collaborative contexts.

This text is intended to help all involved in commissioning:

- understand its distinguishing characteristics;
- appreciate how it continues to be affected by changes in the public sector generally and health and social care in particular;
- recognise its significant potential to improve service quality and value for money;
- engage in productive conversations that will lead to better outcomes for patients, clients and the community.

The content of this text is informed by the authors' shared beliefs that:

- at its most powerful, commissioning is a form of whole-system strategic management involving collaboration between public sector organisations, companies, the voluntary sector, service users and citizens;
- commissioning is a process by which health and wellbeing outcomes can be improved and the outlook for individuals and communities transformed;
- whilst commissioning has much to offer individual public sector organisations, its real impact will only be felt when this is undertaken in collaboration across the whole community;
- commissioning is not the same as purchasing or procurement – it is a more strategic, collaborative process that requires creativity, strategic thinking, performance management and technical and leadership competence to enable continuous improvement;
- all health and social care stakeholders need to understand and participate in commissioning – it is not a process that should be limited to planners or business managers working in commissioning organisations;
- GPs, social workers and other professionals, whether involved in provision or commissioning, need to develop associated technical competencies as well as be able to practise leadership in new collaborative contexts;
- an awareness of self and self leadership is vital for collaboration, effective commissioning and high performance;
- the capacity to create resonance in others is vital to leading a high-performing service, organisation, cluster and community.

It remains to be seen whether the parallel development of the two worlds of the NHS and social care will continue to be parallel or whether they may, at some point, converge. In our view, for the sake of delivering the best, integrated support to our population, we hope that convergence will win out in the end – we need the best of both worlds.

Chapter 2
Introduction to commissioning

CHAPTER OBJECTIVES

By the end of this chapter you should be able to:

- define commissioning and appreciate the potential benefits of this approach to public service leadership;
- understand the origins of commissioning and how it compares with other management processes;
- appreciate key commissioning roles and relationships;
- understand the importance of collaboration to successful commissioning, alternative approaches and key activities.

What is commissioning?

To some extent the public sector has always undertaken activities associated with commissioning, not always very well or necessarily in an integrated way. This is changing. The last 30 years have seen organisations, structures, relationships, processes and behaviours evolve in ways that encourage and facilitate commissioning. Increasingly, commissioning has been associated with joint working or collaboration within, between and beyond public sector organisations. Understanding of commissioning has developed and continues to evolve in response to shifts in the wider environment and experience.

Commissioning has developed at different speeds and in different ways across the public sector. Currently, a range of approaches can be seen, including those that:

- are little more than advanced procurement;
- are ad hoc, yet quite sophisticated commissioning events or projects;
- are, or will become, embedded. For example, Essex County Council has declared its intention to become commissioning-led (Gordon and Probert 2012: 33).

Varying definitions of commissioning reflect this range of approaches and the characteristics of different parts of the public sector, as shown in Table 2.1.

Table 2.1 Commissioning definitions

The Institute of Commissioning, quoted by the Institute for Government, defines commissioning as: *securing the services that most appropriately address the needs and wishes of the individual service user, making use of market intelligence and research and planning accordingly* (Institute for Government 2010: 4).

The Audit Commission defines commissioning as: *the process of specifying, securing and monitoring services to meet people's needs at a strategic level. This applies to all services, whether they are provided by the local authority, NHS or other public agencies or by the private or voluntary sectors* (Care Services Improvement Partnership 2006: 2).

The Department for Communities and Local Government (2009: 9) considers commissioning as being: *the means to secure best value and deliver the positive outcomes that meet the needs of citizens, communities and service users.*

Commissioning by Children's Trusts has been defined as: *the process for deciding how to use the total resource available for children, young people and parents in order to improve outcomes in the most efficient, effective, equitable and sustainable way* (Commissioning Support Programme 2009: 3).

The National Offender Management Service sees commissioning as: *the cycle of assessing the needs of courts, offenders, defendants, victims and communities then designing, securing and monitoring services to meet those needs, while making the best use of total available resources* (Ministry of Justice 2011: 3).

In 2007 the NHS introduced World Class Commissioning, in respect of which the core task of Primary Care Trusts (PCTs) was stated as being to: *invest locally to achieve the greatest health gains and reductions in health inequalities, at best value for current and future service users* (Department of Health 2007d: 1).

With the demise of PCTs and the advent of Clinical Commissioning Groups, commissioning is now seen as: *the process of arranging continuously improving services which deliver the best possible quality and outcomes for patients, meet the population's health needs and reduce inequalities within the resources available* (NHS Commissioning Board 2012: 5).

Similarities between definitions suggest that commissioning:

- is a cycle rather than an event;
- should be driven by needs and outcomes;
- is a whole process involving specifying need, securing supply and monitoring outcomes;
- should result in continuous improvement and best value;
- is strategic in nature and undertaken on behalf of a client group, locality or community.

The last point is debatable for, although commissioning is often strategic in nature, there is a view that it can apply at different levels, including that of individual service users. The Confederation of British Industry (CBI) and the Local

Government Association (LGA) identify at least five levels at which public sector commissioning occurs (CBI/LGA 2009: 10): individual, locality, service, strategic and regional/national, whilst the Department of Health suggests three levels: citizen, operational and strategic, with the overall aim being to *empower citizens with support needs to make use of, and further develop their capacity to self-direct their care, and where possible, to directly shape the support they receive* (Department of Health 2010c: 16).

For many organisations, the application of commissioning is becoming more strategic. For example, joint commissioning involves *two or more agencies pooling their resources to implement a common strategy for providing services* (Audit Commission 1998: 2) and collaborative commissioning with *two or more agencies coordinating their strategies for using their resources* (Audit Commission 1998: 2).

Key roles

Historically, public sector organisations delivered many services 'in house'. Services provided direct to clients, such as older people's services in local authorities, tended to be grouped so they could be more easily managed. Frequently, support activities that could have been contracted from the private sector were also provided in house, such as cleaning and gardening. The manager of a residential home, for example, would have no option but to employ and manage a gardener, rather than enter into a grounds maintenance contract with a provider. Over the years, in-house activities such as catering and cleaning have been market-tested and many of these are now provided by contractors. More recently, even the services these activities used to support are likely to have been outsourced.

Commissioning has caused two roles to emerge – commissioning and providing – and the relationship between these two roles is critical to long-term success.

Those *commissioning* have traditionally been referred to as clients or purchasers, a role which in the early days focused on purchasing services and managing contacts. They would be assisted by procurement and contract management specialists.

Those *providing* services, traditionally referred to as suppliers, contractors or providers, fulfilled a role that, in the early days, focused on service delivery in accordance with a contract or service level agreement. The terms 'supplier' or 'contractor' are typically associated with organisations that are external to the commissioning organisation, whilst 'provider' can be used to describe internal or external organisations.

Over the years, the respective roles of commissioners and providers have been expanded, as detailed in later sections.

One common myth of commissioning is that it brings to an end internal provision, whereas it should lead to provision by the most appropriate provider. In practice, the nature of many public services requires some internal provision and, therefore, a mixed economy is necessary.

The commissioning landscape is potentially complex as organisations respond to pressure to reduce expenditure by collaborating, sharing and providing services to each other. It is quite possible that an organisation may, at the same time, commission:

- services they are responsible for on behalf of their local community;
- services with other agencies on behalf of their local community;
- another agency to commission services on their behalf;
- prime contractors to manage the detailed commissioning process, sometimes referred to as integrated commissioning – as with the Department for Work and Pensions, which in 2008 signalled its intent to create *a stronger, more consistent base of top-tier providers who can work closely with regional and sub-regional partners to deliver sustainable jobs for unemployed people* (Department for Work and Pensions 2008: 9);

and provide:

- services to itself whilst purchasing the rest from other public, private and voluntary sector organisations;
- services to other public service organisations within or outside their community;
- commissioning support to other public service organisations within or outside their community.

Benefits from commissioning

Service design and delivery have traditionally been influenced, if not driven, by professionals employed by individual public agencies. Vested interests in maintaining existing patterns of provision together with relatively short planning and budget cycles make it likely the status quo will be maintained. The result is that:

- service users with needs that are currently being met will continue to have them met;
- existing services will continue in the same way, delivered by current providers;
- value for money is likely to be lower than it could be.

By comparison, commissioning should be a constant process, routinely involving challenging which needs will be met and how.

TIPS FOR SUCCESS

In order to challenge the status quo successfully and improve service user outcomes, a number of factors have to come into play.

- *Managers need to 'really' understand the felt needs of clients and other stakeholders.*

> - *Responsibility for creativity in general, and innovation in particular, should be shared by commissioners and providers.*
> - *Commissioners and providers need to be able to use creativity processes and tools, and harness the natural diversity present amongst stakeholders.*

Commissioning done well, particularly when undertaken in collaboration:

- prompts service users and citizen engagement;
- removes complacency and prompts innovation;
- leads to better responses to population need and outcomes;
- encourages intelligence sharing to improve the whole system;
- provides a framework for using potentially transformational techniques;
- encourages conversation between different stakeholders;
- sharpens accountability and performance reporting;
- prompts greater economy, efficiency and effectiveness through choice and competition;
- encourages better understanding of cost;
- is a catalyst for performance improvement, service flexibility and change;
- enables a more integrated set of services that are seamless for users, producing outcomes that are more than the sum of providers' activities;
- involves decisions based on evidence of need and understanding of what works rather than what has always been provided.

CASE STUDY 2.1

Essex County Council floating support contract

In April 2012, Essex County Council realised 5.8 per cent cashable savings, a 6.9 per cent increase in the number of support hours delivered each year and increased workforce flexibility through reletting two floating support contracts with a total annual value of £5m. These contracts were funded through Housing Related Support (previously Supporting People) and retendered through a commissioning process that took account of:

- *emerging needs regarding vulnerable young people and mental health users that might require the size of floating support contracts to grow;*
- *the possibility that further specialisms might also need floating support in future;*
- *an opportunity for an existing Housing Related Support direct payments scheme to be brought within the contract;*

- an opportunity for a contract currently held by an organisation wishing to with-draw from Housing Related Support provision also to be transferred in, whilst widening the target group to vulnerable older people with support needs;
- a potential for increased use by volunteers of person-centred practice to increase user independence and achieve outcomes within an identified time-scale, rather than create dependency;
- potential economies of operation that could be gained through joint commis-sioning with a neighbouring authority.

Understanding and integrating these factors led commissioners to:

- specify that they required a holistic service;
- identify the minimum size of contract required to meet identified needs whilst at the same time signalling that this might increase;
- alert providers to the possibility that in future they might be asked to:
  - o offer new services;
  - o work with new specialisms;
  - o increase delivery volumes;
  - o offer greater intensity of services to service users experiencing particular life events, e.g. death of a carer.

TIPS FOR SUCCESS

The success of this example of good commissioning is due to those involved:

- taking time to gather and synthesise information regarding:
  - o the environment within which future social and health outcomes will need to be addressed;
  - o the numbers of future potential service users, patterns and trends;
  - o the effectiveness of different ways of meeting outcomes;
  - o how professional practice is changing;
  - o the number of existing providers, performance and future intentions;
- using tools and processes to develop strategic thinking, challenge assumptions and stimulate new ideas;
- appropriately sharing thinking and commissioning intentions with providers;
- ensuring strategic thinking led to strategic decision making and ultimately informed procurement.

Commissioning compared with other management processes

Commissioning is similar to, but differs from, established management processes such as business and service planning, procurement, contracting, business process improvement and strategic management.

Business and service planning is the *process by which a desired future state is conceived and an effective way of delivering this developed and resourced* (Field 2012: 2). Commissioning involves analysis, direction setting and action planning, and utilises many of the techniques used by planners. It also tends to place greater emphasis on the community and on implementation and review.

Public procurement is the *process of the acquisition, usually by means of a contractual arrangement after public competition, of goods, services, works and other supplies by the public service* (Central Procurement Directorate 2012: 4). Defined this way, procurement can be seen to be part of the commissioning process. The Association of Chief Executives of Voluntary Organisations (ACEVO) explains that procurement is *the specific aspects of the commissioning cycle that focus on the process of buying services from initial advertising through to appropriate contract arrangements* (ACEVO 2012: 3). However, it should be noted that this view of commissioning and procurement is far from universal; terms such as 'intelligent' and 'strategic' procurement indicate considerable variation in practice. Sir Peter Gershon, Chief Executive of the Office of Government Commerce, defines procurement as:

> the whole process of acquisition from third parties (including logistical aspects) and covers goods, services and construction projects. This process spans the whole life cycle from initial concept and definition of business needs through to the end of the useful life of an asset or the end of a services contract.

> (National Audit Office 2012a: 2)

Over the last two or three decades, the public sector has pursued step and continuous improvement using a variety of approaches, such as the business excellence model, business process re-engineering, lean thinking, pathway redesign and results-based accountability. Where culturally embedded, these approaches share many of the characteristics of commissioning but may still lack the width and depth of coverage.

Of all the established processes, strategic management is the one to which commissioning is perhaps closest. This can be defined as the:

> process by which organisations determine their purpose, objectives and desired levels of attainment, decide on actions for achieving their objectives in an appropriate timescale, and frequently in a changing environment; implement the actions; and assess progress and results.

> (Thompson 1997: 6)

9

Strategic management and commissioning are, in most contexts, strategic in nature and wide in scope. However, while commissioning tends to focus on outcome achievement for patients, clients and the community, strategic management is more concerned with organisational success. Whilst the two are clearly linked, this is an important distinction.

Another way of looking at commissioning is that it is an amalgam of management processes pursued in a way that can result in significant benefit. In practice, the leaders of each organisation will define what commissioning means to them in terms of scope, frameworks, processes and, more widely, culture.

Where does commissioning come from?

The activities, behaviours and skills associated with commissioning are long established in the public sector. However, as a term and a 'whole process', commissioning really emerged in the late 1980s. Glasby, reporting Walters, makes the point that in 1988 commissioning was only mentioned 12 times in *Hansard*, compared to 1,000 times in 2007 (Glasby 2012: 21).

Since 1979, when Margaret Thatcher came to power, successive governments have fought to address developments in the wider environment and the pace of resultant change has quickened. Successive Conservative, Labour and coalition governments have either directly promoted commissioning or indirectly stimulated a context where it could flourish. Direct actions include initiatives such as World Class Commissioning and the Health and Social Care Act 2012. The Private Finance Initiative, Local Strategic Partnerships and Community Budgeting are examples of government actions that have helped create a potentially 'commissioning-friendly' context. These actions link to five significant drivers: higher performance, a more commercial paradigm, greater private sector involvement, collaboration, and local and individual involvement. In turn, these drivers are influenced by wider environmental factors, particularly those of an economic, political and sociological nature (Figure 2.1).

Higher performance

There are insufficient public funds to meet all the needs within a community. It is important, therefore, that public service organisations demonstrate best use of resources. The last 30 years have seen a stream of initiatives that have encouraged higher performance. Examples include Value for Money, one of five tasks forming Margaret Thatcher's 1979 manifesto; Best Value (Local Government Act 1999); the 2004 Gershon Review, which set target savings of £6.5bn and £6.45bn by 2007–2008 for the Department of Health and local government respectively; and Quality, Innovation, Productivity and Prevention (QIPP), to enable the NHS to save £20bn over three years to 2014. The introduction of the Comprehensive Performance Assessment in 2002, which morphed into the Comprehensive Area Assessment in 2009, the setting of a

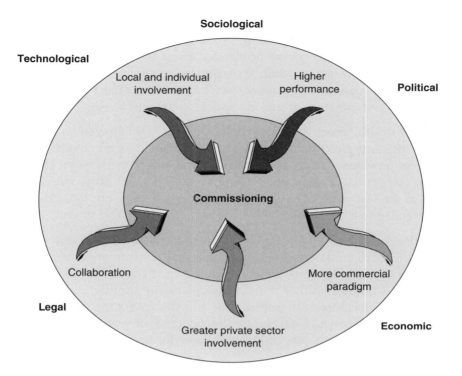

Figure 2.1 Commissioning environment

plethora of targets and performance indicators, inspections, publication of league tables and reports has been a significant feature of the public sector landscape in recent years. Since 2010, the coalition government has abolished the Audit Commission, scrapped the Comprehensive Area Assessment process and reduced the number of performance indicators. Pressure on performance has, however, been maintained through significant reductions in public spending and increased accountability regarding spending. The introduction of the employee's 'right to provide' and the community's 'right to challenge' to run public services applies pressure on public agencies to perform, whilst giving opportunities for social enterprises and groups, such as community associations, to run local services.

More commercial paradigm

The Local Government Planning and Land Act 1980 introduced compulsory competitive tendering (CCT), challenging the assumption that activities such as construction, maintenance and highways work should automatically be undertaken by local authority staff. The scope of CCT was extended to support services in health authorities in 1982 and by 1996 refuse collection, ground maintenance, sports and leisure management, legal, property and personnel services within public sector organisations also came under the legislation. CCT brought into being the 'client role' within local authorities, with contracts let on a competitive basis to private sector companies or internal direct labour organisations (DLOs). Whilst CCT was abolished in 1999, the expectation that services would need to compete and be compared or market-tested against others carried into Best Value and remains a feature of public sector leadership.

The National Health Service and Community Care Act 1990 created an internal market in the NHS with health authorities and GP fundholders purchasing healthcare from internal providers, such as acute hospitals and ambulance services, that were to operate in competition as independent NHS trusts. This was followed in 2004 by the approval of the first wave of Foundation Trusts as self-standing, independent legal entities intended to enjoy considerable freedom and accountable to local people.

CCT and the creation of an internal health market shifted public sector organisations toward more commercial ways of operating. Performance measures, such as return on capital employed, were introduced for DLOs, trading accounts were developed and business rather than service planning adopted. In many organisations, this more commercial approach led to the formation of business units, budget decentralisation and devolution, introduction of service level agreements, internal recharging and the use of business cases for decision making.

Greater private sector involvement

The 1980s was a period of significant change for the UK. The Thatcher administration embarked on a series of initiatives which opened up the market to greater private sector involvement. Deregulation and the privatisation of British Telecom, British Gas, British Airways, Rolls-Royce, the British Airports Authority and others reduced the scale and breadth of the public sector and widened share ownership. During the same period, council house tenants were given the right to buy their homes at a discount.

In 1992, John Major's administration introduced the Private Finance Initiative, which, in effect, became the only way of financing capital spend – another step in the journey to opening up public sector organisations to working with the private sector. In 2000, Labour agreed to send NHS patients for treatment in independent hospitals and, in 2002, invited private health companies to compete to run independent sector treatment centres specialising in routine day surgery.

The 'right to provide' by state employees is one of the latest attempts to open up more public services to private practice, this time through encouraging the creation of social enterprises.

Collaboration

In recent years, local authorities, health and other agencies have increasingly been expected to collaborate at a strategic and operational level. Examples include the 1999 Health Act, which introduced new flexibilities such as pooled budgeting, lead commissioning and integrated provision, and the 2003 Community Care Act, which made local authorities financially responsible if arrangements were not in place to allow patients to be discharged from hospital. The drive to collaborate extends beyond health and adult social care and, during Tony Blair's administration, Children's Trusts, Youth Offending Teams, Local Strategic Partnerships and other joint bodies were established. Collaboration has been promoted as a means of achieving greater economy and efficiency, improving service outcomes and addressing 'wicked' issues in an integrated way.

In December 2011, the Local Government Secretary Eric Pickles announced Whole-Place Community Budget pilots as a means by which red tape could be cut, policy making improved and public sector financial savings made. During 2012, joint teams of local agencies, supplemented by government officials, proposed ways in which decision making and budgets could be devolved. Community budgeting is a way of giving local public service partners freedom to collaborate on service redesign focused on improving outcomes and the needs of citizens. It is expected that community budgets will give local people control over local services and make better use of pooled resources from across the communities.

The journey to increased collaboration continues with David Cameron's coalition government, a notable example of which is the Health and Social Care Act 2012, which introduced Health and Wellbeing Boards and a duty to undertake a Joint Strategic Needs Assessment and prepare a Joint Commissioning Strategy.

Local and individual involvement

On assuming power in 2010, Prime Minister David Cameron embarked on a series of measures intended to reduce centralised bureaucracy and encourage local and individual involvement. A Minister of State for Decentralisation was appointed and, in a speech in Liverpool in July 2010, the Prime Minister set out the principle of localism:

> We've got to get rid of the centralised bureaucracy that wastes money and undermines morale and in its place we've got to . . . open up public services to new providers . . . So we get more innovation, diversity and responsiveness to public need. We need to create communities with oomph – neighbourhoods who are in charge of their own destiny, who feel if they club together and get involved they can shape the world around them.

(www.britishpoliticalspeeches.org/speech-acrhive.htm?speech=32)

The Localism Act 2011 introduced a number of measures to give town halls greater discretion about responding to local communities. It made the planning system more responsive to these communities which would also have the right to challenge to take over the running of local services.

By encouraging communities to find their voice and enabling local authorities to respond more flexibly, interest has been stimulated in identifying and meeting local need. Both of these factors are an integral part of successful commissioning.

In health and social care, there has been considerable interest in helping patients and clients identify need, articulate, plan and manage their care. Choose and Book, direct payments, individual budgets and, more generally, personalisation encourage individuals to be more actively engaged in their own care. This shift challenges traditional views of the role of public services.

Successful commissioning – collaboration

Successful commissioning requires key activities and processes to be completed to a high standard, which in turn requires a mix of professional and managerial skills. Treating these activities simply as a set of transactions will not release the full potential of commissioning. Commissioning is a process that requires a web of good-quality relationships between patients, clients, commissioners, providers and the community.

Many commissioning models and related competence frameworks use the language of engagement to describe the relationship between commissioners and the community. Engagement is vitally important to effective commissioning. The early emphasis on engagement signalled a shift from professionals determining services to be provided to citizens articulating need and priorities, then influencing how these should be met. However, engagement does not adequately describe the sort of relationships that will be needed in future. Across the community, robust conversations are required about need and service prioritisation, behaviour change, co-production and co-financing. Active involvement of individuals and community bodies will be necessary; collaborating to achieve the very best outcomes.

The quality of relationships between commissioners and providers differs significantly, as identified by the Institute of Public Care and quoted by the Care Services Improvement Partnership (2007b: 8), and shown in Figure 2.2.

Both adversarial and passive relationships have positive features; however, neither is ideal. Adversarial relationships are good in that commissioners actively

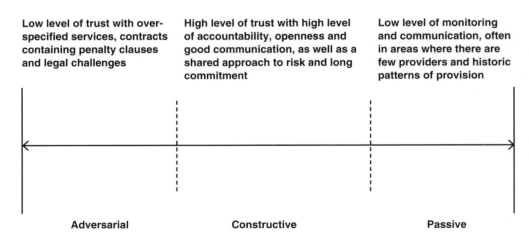

Figure 2.2 Relationship spectrum

engage in the commissioning process and providers are challenged to improve and perform. However, the cost of letting contracts, monitoring and compliance, potential inflexibility and the demotivating effect of micro-control can shift attention from service delivery to contract management. Passive relationships, by contrast, can lead to situations where providers are not sufficiently challenged to improve performance and commissioners fail to develop intelligence about providers and service efficacy, leading to poor value for money. Constructive relationships are needed between commissioners and providers so as to ensure:

- appropriate pressure is applied to improve performance;
- intelligence is gathered and shared;
- appropriate financial returns can be made;
- innovation occurs;
- contract management costs are acceptable;
- flexibility and trust are present.

Relationships need to be more than just constructive. They need to be collaborative with commissioners and providers working together to deliver on behalf of the community, achieving their own goals and contributing to the goals of each other.

Increasingly, public sector organisations are expected to work together to commission, a trend which has generated a plethora of terms such as lead commissioning, joint commissioning and, perhaps, most importantly, partnership. Despite recent widespread use, the term partnership is not actually the most appropriate or helpful. As the Audit Commission (1998: 16) concluded, *partnership is a slippery concept that is difficult to define precisely*. There are varying understandings of what this term means, flowing from its traditional use to describe either an organisational form or a type of relationship. Neither of these is entirely helpful in describing arrangements which may involve unequal power and authority, lack a distinct legal form and involve compulsory participation. Recently, the term collaboration rather than partnership has come to the fore to describe how people work together. This has been defined as *the process of facilitating and operating in multi-organisational arrangements to address challenges that cannot be solved or easily solved by single organisations* (InWent 2009: 16).

Attention to service user pathways, joined-up approaches to meeting need and commissioning in respect of larger geographic areas require a combination and scale of provision that will increasingly require several providers. Achieving best value from these services requires more than coordination. Providers need to find ways of collaborating on projects and services to achieve best outcomes whilst recognising they might at the same time be competing for other work.

Before commissioning became commonplace, public sector organisations tended to provide services that professional staff believed necessary. Little changed with early commissioning, where public sector organisations contracted for services its professionals believed were needed. Commissioning has evolved to the point where public sector leaders engage with the community to identify the services needed and then contract with providers. The next step will see public sector leaders collaborating with the community to identify and prioritise need, develop strategies to reduce avoidable need through, for example, behaviour change, responding to remaining need through self-help, third-party help and, as a last resort, publicly funded delivery via the most appropriate provider.

Collaboration is key to successful long-term commissioning and characteristically will include shared values, a level playing field for providers of all sizes, mutual respect and robust conversations about performance, cost recovery and price. Today's public service context demands 360-degree collaboration involving community members, commissioning organisations and providers.

TIPS FOR SUCCESS

In order to create and maintain productive long-term relationships:

- *commissioners and providers need to develop a shared vision with the community and clients;*

- *there needs to be a shared understanding of what commissioners and providers have in common as well as recognition and celebration of different perspectives, motivations and priorities;*

- *conversation that is supportive and developmental, whilst at the same time challenging, needs to be encouraged. Ultimately, these conversations and relationships in general should be underpinned by an appropriate contract.*

The commissioning process – a model

Various models of commissioning exist across the public sector, normally presented as stages and activities, the number and names of which vary. At a high level, the National Offender Management Service (Ministry of Justice 2011: 19) uses a three-stage commissioning cycle, as set out in Table 2.2.

Table 2.2 Commissioning model – National Offender Management Service

Stage	Involves
Planning	Understanding need and demand for services, analysing gaps, prioritising and deprioritising services and designing services to meet needs
Purchasing	Understanding the market for services and agreeing a strategy for securing them, including alignment of resources with other commissioners
Performance management	Gaining assurance that service providers deliver expected outcomes, strive for continuous improvement and manage delivery chains effectively and fairly

The Department for Work and Pensions commissioning cycle (Glasby 2012: 26) also comprises three stages (Table 2.3).

The Department for Children, Schools and Families (now called the Department for Education) presented commissioning as a four-stage model (Commissioning Support Programme 2010: 8) (Table 2.4).

The NHS Information Centre (2008) presents World Class Commissioning as a three-stage model (Table 2.5).

Table 2.3 Commissioning model – Department for Work and Pensions

Stage	Involves
Plan	Demand analysis, market capacity analysis, resource analysis, risk analysis, strategic planning and contract design
Execute	Contract implementation, provider development
Manage	Contract management and performance management

Table 2.4 Commissioning model – Department for Children, Schools and Families

Stage	Involves
Understand	Recognise the outcomes you want to achieve, identify local needs, resources and priorities and agree what the desired end product should be
Plan	Map out and consider different ways of addressing the needs identified through the needs assessment above
Do	Make investment decisions based on the appropriate action identified in the 'plan' stage to secure delivery of the desired service or services
Review	Monitor service delivery against expected outcomes and report how well it is doing against the plan

Table 2.5 Commissioning model – World Class Commissioning

Stage	Involves
Strategic planning	Assessing needs, reviewing service provisions and deciding priorities
Procuring services	Designing services, shaping structure of supply, planning capacity and managing demand
Monitoring and evaluation	Supporting patient choice, managing performance and seeking public and patient views

Commissioning – a new model

Looking at emerging commissioning models, 16 key activities are apparent and fall within four clusters: knowledge and strategic thinking, planning, doing and reviewing.

Whilst it is tempting to consider these clusters to be stages in a process, this does not do justice to what is involved and how commissioning should work in practice. Presenting commissioning as stages suggests each one is completed before the next is started and probably occurs at a particular time in the year. There is a risk that undue emphasis is given to generating a glossy strategy or plan, with the requirement to generate this determining the timing of each stage. Whilst inevitably some form of commissioning plan is necessary, this should not dominate the commissioning process.

A better way of presenting commissioning is as a set of activities that occur constantly at the same time. Figure 2.3 presents planning, doing and reviewing clusters as cogs, constantly turning within an environment where knowledge is gathered and strategic thinking takes place.

Commissioning involves the preparation and use of plans which need to be kept up to date. Where commissioners rely solely on a plan written before a year begins,

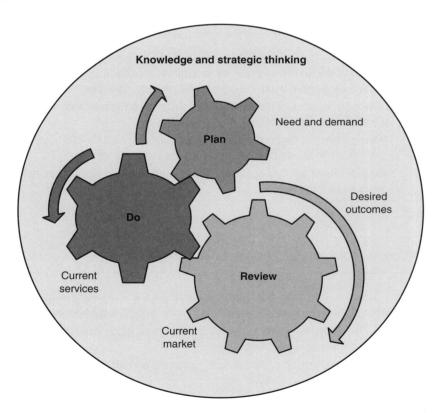

Figure 2.3 A new model of commissioning

they may fail to respond appropriately to changes in the environment and community during that year. In practice, the actions needed to commission continue throughout the year, some undertaken annually, some monthly and others on a daily basis. If commissioners wait to the end of the year to review the achievement of the plan and other key aspects of their work, they run the risk of missing an early opportunity to take action to improve likely outcomes. Periodic review during the year is essential, the frequency of which would be determined by the context.

The knowledge and strategic thinking cluster of activities are similar to the oil in a gear box which, if sufficient and of good quality, will enable the planning, doing and reviewing cogs to run smoothly. Knowledge acquisition, trend and pattern spotting and sense making should be constant features of commissioning. There should be frequent conversations about each person's 'take' on what is happening, what it might mean for commissioning strategy and the actions that might need to be considered. Strategic thinking, which should not be confused with strategic planning, should lead to:

- planning that is quicker and of better quality;
- fine-tuned action;
- reviews that are challenging and informed.

In turn, planning, doing and reviewing activities generate information that should also contribute to the knowledge base in the system and help shape further strategic thinking.

Knowledge and strategic thinking

Four knowledge domains are central to effective commissioning: understanding need and demand, identifying desired outcomes, understanding the current market and understanding current services.

Commissioners need to know what need exists in the community, the number of people with this need, how this need is changing and how important this need is to those affected. Awareness of the total need within a community, the extent to which this is met or unmet and priorities for addressing this are really helpful when making commissioning decisions.

Understanding need is not easy as there are different perspectives.

- Normative need is usually established by a professional based on an assessment informed by training and experience. The risk with this articulation of need is that the map of the world of the professional may be dated and not necessarily coincide with the views of citizens.
- Expressed need is the need that people say they have and may actually state as a want or demand. The risk with identifying need in this way is that people may have limited ambition for public services, may be accustomed to a certain form of service and may not be articulating one or more further needs that are important.

- Felt needs are those which a person may be unaware of or be unable to articulate. These needs may be deep and less obvious, yet have a significant impact.

As an example, if we were present at a community meeting to discuss higher than usual levels of local crime, the following contributions might be heard:

- a senior police officer announcing she will increase the frequency of police car patrols as the number of incidents has reached a level where this usually occurs (normative need);

- a member of the community who demands more police officers on the beat (expressed need);

- another member of the community who says she does not feel able to go out at night, as she feels scared and socially isolated, i.e. she is in fear of crime being committed (felt needs).

Providing beat officers or increasing the use of patrol cars might reduce the level of crime but will not fully address the needs of some community members. It is important when commissioning to suspend normative need and get beneath expressed need. Surfacing and understanding felt need is particularly important with regard to wellbeing. Focusing on felt need is likely to generate energy, unleash creativity and lead to improved outcomes. In the above example, there are many different ways in which an inability to leave the home at night, fear and social isolation can be addressed, many of which will be more effective and less expensive than increasing police patrols.

Commissioners need to know how demand for services and underlying need are changing now and likely to change in the future as a result of shifts in the environment. These shifts can include sociological, political, economic, legal and technological factors.

There is a need to know how demand is created and for commissioners to consider how individuals and communities might minimise the need for publicly funded services. Consideration should be given first to:

- managing expectations;

- encouraging behaviour change and individuals to take personal responsibility;

- helping people to understand what they can do for themselves and where to go for help;

- facilitating people and community organisations to meet need;

- prevention;

- co-production;

and, only then:

- direct state provision, having considered processes for referral, assessment and triage.

One of the distinguishing characteristics of commissioning is the use of outcomes, and those leading the process should ask the following questions:

- At the highest level, what sort of community do citizens wish to live within?
- To what extent is there a gap between this community vision and the current state?
- What actions need to be taken and what outcomes should result?

In order to understand the market, commissioners need to ask a number of questions:

- What is known about resources within the community that could be used more intensively to deliver the vision?
- How many actual and potential providers offer services in our market?
- What is the capacity of the current market and is this sufficient for the future?
- Where are there gaps in provision or supply that is vulnerable?
- Is the market sufficiently competitive?
- What is the balance of power within the market and between commissioners and providers?
- Is there a sufficient number of providers?
- Is there a real choice for users?
- How sound are existing providers?
- Are providers sufficiently innovative?
- Is there sufficient drive for improvement amongst providers?
- What are relationships like between commissioners and providers?

In order to understand services, commissioners need answers to a number of questions:

- Are there sufficient services, products and facilities available to meet current and future need?
- How well do existing services satisfy prioritised needs?
- Are new responses required to address existing or future anticipated needs?
- What is the quality of services available and how does this compare to price?
- What services or products are being developed outside the community and could these be replicated?
- How quickly are technological advances introduced into services and products?
- Are there substitutes that could be considered?
- What evidence is there of the efficacy of services, products and treatments?

Knowledge and strategic thinking require significant data regarding the local population, patterns and trends of need and what works in practice. Commissioners should constantly:

- scan the environment for early signals of changes that might affect their local population as a whole, different communities, their organisation, providers and their staff;

- engage the community to ensure outcomes are the best expression of what commissioners should be striving to achieve;

- assess the market to ensure it remains healthy and problems are avoided;

- review services so they remain relevant and effective.

Planning

By accessing knowledge and strategic thinking, commissioners should have a good understanding of the environment within which they will be commissioning. Planning activities include deciding priorities and identifying different ways of addressing these, designing services and determining the ideally shaped market, together with aligning and allocating resources.

It is unlikely there will be sufficient resources available to achieve all the outcomes required for a community, at least in the very short term. Commissioners therefore must find a way of engaging their community in conversation about priorities (Figure 2.4).

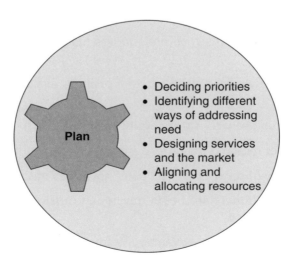

Figure 2.4 Planning activities

There are often different ways of achieving an outcome and meeting one or more needs. Commissioners should find ways of creating space and the opportunity for stakeholders to generate options for meeting needs and challenging the status quo. Arising from this may be proposals for a new service, product or treatment that will need to be designed, piloted and evaluated.

Having prioritised needs, identified different possible responses and developed new services, commissioners will then be in a position to allocate resources in a way that is aligned to them. Taking into consideration resources within the various agencies and wider community, several planning iterations may be necessary to ensure commissioning plans and available resources are in balance.

Doing

Whilst planning on a continual basis, commissioners will also be conducting or 'doing' business as usual (Figure 2.5). Two broad categories are involved: procuring supply and ensuring contract compliance and tackling the strategic challenge of managing demand and the market.

The current commissioning plan should state what is to be commissioned, from where and at what price. Competitive tendering, contractor selection, contract negotiation and agreement are likely to involve procurement specialists. Supply under existing and new contracts will need to be monitored to ensure performance requirements are met and contract terms complied with.

Flowing from the plan and current knowledge of demand, the market place and services, it may be necessary to act to ensure these are managed to achieve

Figure 2.5 Doing activities

the desired outcomes. The commissioning plan may therefore contain actions that are:

- designed to reduce or channel demand for publicly funded services, for example, through educational programmes and preventive investment;

- intended to stimulate and strengthen the market, including, for example, pilot schemes, training and development and provision of information and support;

- aimed at market management, including, for example, ceasing to use a supplier, acting on quality concerns and encouraging new suppliers.

Reviewing

Reviewing activities involve monitoring the impact of commissioning decisions, striving for continuous improvement, reporting performance and learning from it (Figure 2.6).

As with other professional and management activities, commissioning plans need to be monitored regularly. Outcomes are at the heart of commissioning and should be monitored on a regular basis throughout the year. It is important that commissioners understand the impact of particular initiatives, treatment or services so that these can be continued, amended or suspended as appropriate. Outcome achievement should form part of wider performance management, along with other aspects such as budget management. In addition, periodic studies should explore aspects of commissioning in far greater detail and over a longer period.

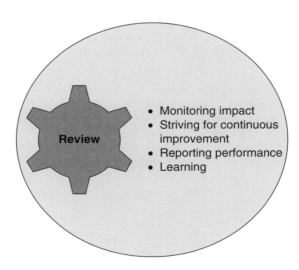

Figure 2.6 Reviewing activities

Commissioning should feature both innovation and adaptive improvement. Innovation involves a preparedness to experiment with new ways of meeting need and novel ways of working and is likely to lead to step improvement in outcomes and performance. Adaptation involves improving what is already being done so that it is faster, cheaper and of a better standard. Both innovation and adaptation, through continuous improvement, should feature throughout the commissioning landscape. Commissioners should strive to get the best possible outcomes with the resources available, creating conditions where they and other stakeholders can perform. Providers should seek continuous improvement as a way of maintaining custom and achieving acceptable financial returns whilst maintaining competitive advantage. Annual or more frequent reviews should require providers to demonstrate actual and planned continuous improvement. This is also an opportunity to identify current or potential problems and find ways to resolve or avoid them.

Regular reporting of performance is important for transparency and accountability reasons and to encourage conversation and idea generation amongst stakeholders.

A culture of learning and continuous improvement, rather than blame, should underpin impact monitoring and reporting which, in turn, should feed into systems and processes used to capture knowledge and stimulate thinking within the community. Beyond this, learning should be shared with, as well as taken from, other communities.

What skills are needed?

A review of commissioning skills or competence frameworks suggests a significant number of skills are needed to play a full and effective part in commissioning. Many of these skills or competencies are general in nature whilst others are clearly identifiable with the commissioning process. Many skills are concerned with what may be referred to as commercial acumen, including, for example, understanding profit and loss accounts, balance sheets and cash flow, using cost and price information, leading the market and individual supplier management. In addition, managers need to be able to read environments, understand competitive behaviour, integrate business information from various sources and exercise judgement.

Given the current financial climate, the number of staff engaged in commissioning, differing levels of experience, prior learning and transferability, the focus for development should be those skills that are either new to participants or where the commissioning context makes it necessary to modify significantly the way these are used.

In addition, skills can be further classified as either transactional in nature, needed in order to undertake commissioning activities, or transformational, that is, concerned with the qualities of relationships, collaboration and how the commissioning process is led.

With regard to transactional skills, which are largely professional or managerial in nature, development should focus on those needed to complete the 16 activities identified earlier.

With regard to transformational skills, which largely concern leadership, development should focus on collaboration – not an entirely new skill, but one that needs to be applied in a new context.

Where existing development options already address commissioning skills, a slight tailoring of these to reflect the commissioning context might be all that is needed. Where existing options do not cover a skill required for commissioning, an appropriate means of development should be designed.

TIPS FOR SUCCESS

In order to ensure that the correct number of competent and confident commissioning and provider managers are available:

- *organisations should adopt a set of competences that reflect the role and responsibilities of staff as determined by the adopted approach to commissioning;*

- *attention should be paid to developing both transactional and transformational skills;*

- *joint development of commissioners and providers should be undertaken to help them understand each other's 'world';*

- *learning by simulation should feature in the approach to development. This helps participants understand the balances and challenges associated with maintaining a healthy commissioning environment and reinforces the importance of transactional and transformational skills.*

Chapter 3
Commissioning in the NHS

CHAPTER OBJECTIVES

By the end of this chapter you should be able to:

- appreciate how commissioning in the NHS has developed since 1990;
- understand the health environment emerging from the Health and Social Care Act 2012;
- understand the journey to authorisation for the new Clinical Commissioning Groups (CCGs) and the challenges of commissioning in this sector.

The development of commissioning in the NHS

England is the only one of the four nations in the UK which uses commissioning as the main means of allocating resources within the NHS, distinguishing between the complementary roles of commissioning and providing services. The fact that England has the best health outcomes but the lowest per capita spend has reinforced this policy approach (National Audit Office 2012b: 7).

Over the last 20 years, commissioning in the NHS has been on a long and tortuous journey and GPs have played a key part during that period. GP-led commissioning is nothing new and many of those GPs emerging in leadership roles within the new CCGs have been involved in the commissioning process, to some degree, for longer than 20 years. The main stages of the journey are outlined below.

GP fundholding

The Conservative government first introduced the option of GP fundholding in the NHS and Community Care Act which was passed in 1990. This enabled GP practices to be offered funds to purchase a limited range of operations and local outpatient services for their patients as well as pay for the drugs they prescribed. The scheme was voluntary and the health authority remained responsible for emergency and more costly complex cases.

Opinions amongst GPs about this approach were divided. However, even those who did not approve could recognise the opportunity which the scheme could give them to restore some of the influence they had over their hospital consultant colleagues before 1948. This concept was introduced at the same time as hospitals, and later mental health, community and ambulance services, were offered the opportunity to become self-managing NHS trusts. Despite the clear opposition led by the British Medical Association (BMA), 306 GP practices had joined the scheme and 57 NHS trusts were established by 1991 (Timmins 2001: 469).

Benefits identified included improved communication between GP practices and hospital consultants, leading to better care (Audit Commission 1996: 14). By 1996, roughly 50 per cent of all GPs had become fundholders. The government decided that it would not force the others to join the scheme. Instead, a number of different models of GP-led commissioning started to develop, including as many as 80 total purchasing pilots (Mays 1997), where fundholders or groups of fundholders were given control of virtually the whole commissioning budget for their area. It has been suggested that they had some success in influencing the pattern of delivery of community care closer to patients' homes (Mays 1997).

In the case of both GP fundholding and total purchasing, any savings made could be retained by the individual GP practices concerned as long as they benefited patients.

There were no national targets during this period. Depending upon where patients lived, the waiting times for 'routine surgery' could be over two years.

Primary care groups

Following election victory in 1997, the Labour government set out its ten-year vision in the White Paper *The New NHS – Modern, Dependable* (Department of

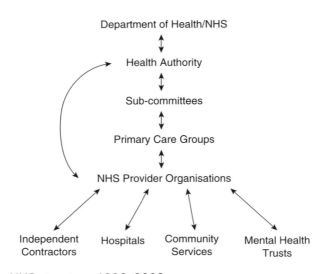

Figure 3.1 The NHS structure 1998–2000

Health 1997). Although they were committed to ending the 'internal market', they retained the division of the respective responsibilities of purchasers and providers for planning and delivering services (Figure 3.1).

The Labour government established 481 Primary Care Groups (PCGs) in the late 1990s to cover the catchment areas of groups of GP practices in recognisable, but relatively small, geographical areas, e.g. Rochester and Strood. These PCGs were officially subcommittees of the 95 health authorities, e.g. West Kent, which existed at the time. They were established to:

- *improve the health of the population in the PCG;*
- *develop primary and community health services;*
- *commission secondary and tertiary services for the population in the PCG.*

(The Health Foundation 2004: 9–10)

They were led by 'boards' of usually five or six GPs and up to three nurses who were elected from amongst the clinicians in the area and included representatives from the local social services. They had an indicative budget and limited management support.

Primary Care Trusts

The NHS Plan (Department of Health 2000) confirmed that all PCGs would become PCTs by April 2004. This was brought forward by the *Shifting the Balance of Power* report (Department of Health 2001) and the first PCTs were established by April 2002. Formed from the grouping together of PCGs covering larger geographical areas, each PCT was allocated statutory responsibility for a budget of about £250mn for an average population size of 250,000 (Figure 3.2).

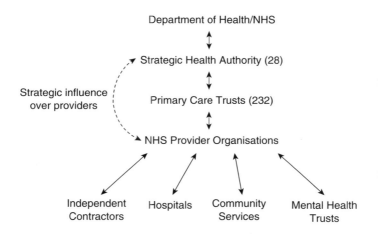

Figure 3.2 The NHS structure 2000–2005

Shifting the balance of power referred to several challenges: the shift away from centralised control to local commissioning, the shift towards clinical teams having greater control in provider organisations, the shift towards more integration of health and social care by giving local authorities greater influence over the NHS and the shift towards the public and patients having more control over their own care.

The report defined PCTs as:

> *primarily local organisations with a focus on the empowerment of clinical teams, local communities and patients, maximising the potential of partnership working, ensuring that the right parties are engaged in decision-making, that decisions are made as close to patients as possible and in an open and inclusive manner.*

(Department of Health 2001: 39)

As a trust, the organisation had to be a separate legal entity, no longer part of the health authority. As such, it was required to have a legally constituted board of executive and non-executive directors. The previous clinically led board 'morphed' into a Professional Executive Committee (PEC), still clinically led (usually by a GP) but reporting into and advising the new PCT board. Clinicians' influence was diluted as a result. Also, when the PECs were set up, they were required to have a broader multi-professional membership, including allied health professionals such as physiotherapists, community pharmacists, dentists and dieticians, some of whom were elected as PEC chairs, instead of GPs.

The main functions of a PCT were defined as management of primary care contracts and community services, public health and commissioning of acute, mental health and tertiary services. The bulk of the staff employed by the PCTs worked in the community services or 'provider arm', whereas often fewer than ten staff would be employed in the Commissioning Directorate, despite the fact that it was responsible for most of the PCT's budget. The lack of clinical focus and 'heavyweight' investment in negotiating power and resources for commissioning made the challenge of 'shifting the balance of power' from secondary to primary care a difficult one. Their role in provider development to achieve a 'plurality of provision' (Department of Health 2000) was often interpreted narrowly as being about the development of their in-house community services provider rather than developing the whole market.

The key leaders of the PCT were seen to be the Chair of the Board, who would be a non-executive director; the Chief Executive, who would have overall responsibility for the organisation; and the Chair of the Professional or Clinical Executive Committee (usually a GP), who would provide clinical direction and advice. These were known initially as the 'three at the top', later redefined more democratically as the 'three at the centre', and between them contributed respectively a strategic, operational and clinical perspective.

It became clear that PCTs needed to collaborate more effectively and, in a number of geographic areas, one PCT would be chosen to lead the commissioning of a given acute hospital or mental health trust to negotiate and manage the contract on behalf of a group of PCTs. Some started to merge voluntarily to strengthen their ability to negotiate, especially where they shared the same acute provider.

At the same time, health authorities were combined into 28 newly named Strategic Health Authorities (SHAs) covering a wider geographical boundary than before, e.g. Kent and Medway.

Early commissioning of private sector hospitals for specific initiatives was used to reduce waiting lists for specific procedures, such as elective surgery (Department of Health 2005a). National targets continued to dominate the commissioning agenda rather than patients' health needs. Many of the larger provider organisations tended to operate as if they were working directly for the Department of Health because of the growing political and media focus on the achievement of national targets and standards (Civitas 2010: 32). The trend towards more locally driven commissioning tended to be undermined by the increasing centrally driven control by the Department of Health.

In 2001, the National Performance Framework was established to include a system of published 'star ratings'. National targets were championed by Alan Milburn, the Secretary of State for Health at that time, and phrases such as 'four hours in A&E' and '18 weeks from referral to treatment' were born.

The NHS Plan (Department of Health 2000) also strengthened the position of local councils by redefining their role as promoting the economic, environment and social wellbeing of their population; in other words, health in the broadest sense. They were also given the power to overview and scrutinise local health services, lead consultation on service reconfiguration and, through their multi-agency Local Strategic Partnership, lead on the development and implementation of long-term plans to improve the local quality of life of their local population.

The Health and Social Care Act 2003 introduced the concept of Foundation Trusts and the first Foundation Trust hospitals were established in 2004. This enabled those higher-performing NHS trusts to apply to become public benefit organisations which would have greater accountability to their local catchment areas. Their governance structure comprises members, drawn from the public and staff, and governors, who are either elected by the public and staff or appointed by local partner organisations. The prize was, and still is, greater autonomy over the management of their income and assets, enabling them to reinvest any surplus they save. It enabled them to form strategic alliances and to retain the right to generate their existing level of private income, if they had any. They would be authorised and regularly assessed by a new arm's-length, national regulator, known as Monitor. This tended to reinforce the attitude of many that their main 'master' was at a national rather than local level (Civitas 2010: 32), rather than recognising the importance of their obligations to their local PCT commissioners. For many, their principal focus simply shifted from the Department of Health to Monitor.

Larger Primary Care Trusts and the introduction of practice-based commissioning

By 2005–2006, it was evident that the investment in hospital-based services had increased rather than decreased and hospital overspends were becoming increasingly common. PCTs were considered to be too small to be effective commissioners, particularly of the larger hospital and mental health trusts. Therefore, it was decided that many should be combined to commission on behalf of a larger population, giving them a greater number of commissioning staff but an even bigger budget to manage; as a result, the number of PCTs reduced from 238 to 152 (Department of Health 2005b) (Figure 3.3).

In many cases, their boundaries were changed to match those of the county council who were responsible for social care, e.g. Cambridgeshire. Where a PCT already shared the same geographical boundary with its local unitary or single-tier council, they remained unchanged, e.g. Southampton.

The link with the local county or unitary council also strengthened further with the agreement that PCT Directors of Public Health should be jointly funded by the local authority and the development of strategic partnerships to oversee services for children and older people. In many cases, collaboration between the PCT and council as joint or co-commissioners became even stronger, with some areas agreeing to set up single management teams, e.g. Tower Hamlets and Southwark, or to appoint a single Chief Executive, e.g. Herefordshire.

Through the Department of Health publication *Transforming Community Services* in 2006, there was a clear directive for PCT commissioners to divest themselves of any direct responsibilities for providing community services. They were expected to put separate governance structures in place for their respective commissioning

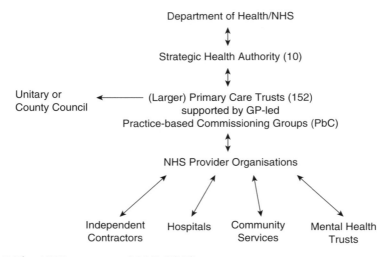

Figure 3.3 The NHS structure 2005–2010

and provision responsibilities with a view to the latter being dis-integrated from the PCT within a two- to three-year timescale.

The three options available to community service organisations were:

1. to become Foundation Trusts in their own right;

2. to merge with an established mental health or hospital Foundation Trust;

3. to become a social enterprise.

In a number of areas, progress was quite slow. In the months leading to the 2010 election, the pressure to complete the dis-integration of community services was increased significantly. For many, the quickest, but not necessarily the easiest, option was to merge with the local mental health trust, as they did in Oxfordshire (Competition and Co-operation Panel 2010).

The Department of Health continued to exert pressure on PCTs to deliver national targets such as 18 weeks between referral and treatment, four-hour waits in Accident and Emergency and the two-week cancer appointments between referral and diagnosis.

By 2005–2006, it had started to become clear that some PCTs' lack of effectiveness had been due to insufficient commissioning resources or expertise. In response to this, the Department of Health (2007c) developed a Framework for World Class Commissioning, in conjunction with McKinsey Consulting. This was intended to provide a means for PCTs to be able both to assess their own performance and to be assessed by the SHA in respect of their commissioning competence. Each PCT was required to rate itself on a scale from one to four, with four being the highest. The results were published annually and very few PCTs were rated above a two, especially those in areas of serious overspend.

This helped to strengthen the view – long held by some – that effective commissioning requires a considerable amount of skill and knowledge and strong clinical input. Many PCTs invested in training and development and recruited more people to resource the function, many of whom had clinical backgrounds.

The clinically led Professional Executive Committees were retained and strengthened by formally being made a subcommittee of the new PCT boards (Department of Health 2007a). It was their duty to provide clinical direction; advise the board on clinical matters, particularly clinical priorities and service development; and also to oversee the development of practice-based commissioning.

The publication of *Commissioning a Patient-Led NHS* (Department of Health 2005b) required PCTs to *make arrangements for 100% coverage of practice based commissioning by no later than the end of 2006*, adding that *individual practices will have the option to take on commissioning to a greater or lesser extent depending on their wishes and their capabilities.*

Practice-based commissioning was intended to enable groups of GP practices to work together across a recognised community area, which was often exactly the same boundary as the original PCG. Their role was to inform the PCT about local needs and help develop more community-based services as alternatives to those in secondary care, especially for long-term conditions care. It would have been more accurate to call them Locality or Area-based Commissioning Groups.

Once again, like fundholding, there was a mixed reception to this concept and, as it was voluntary, the level of interest shown by GPs varied. Some were very entrepreneurial, developing 'clinical villages' providing a wide range of better, local services; some did not engage at all. Throughout this period of greater clinical involvement in commissioning and PCT leadership, the responsibility for the contract, budget and accountability for performance management remained with the PCT.

The SHAs were once again reduced, this time from 28 to 10, to form leaner organisations covering an even wider area, e.g. Kent, Surrey and Sussex, known as South East Coast SHA or NHS South East Coast. Their role was a combination of, firstly, performance management of health economies, principally through PCTs, to ensure that targets were met and budgets well managed and, secondly, capacity building and strategic development to ensure that health economies had the skills and innovation to make best use of their resources, both physical and human. They also started to buy in expertise from central government and the private sector to develop procurement hubs which could provide PCT commissioners with specialist expertise about tendering and contract management.

Recognition of the value of the separation between commissioners and providers was reflected by Lord Darzi in the Department of Health final report, entitled *High Quality Care for All: NHS Next Stage Review* (Department of Health 2008). Lord Darzi also helped to raise the importance of clinical quality alongside value for money. In the Department of Health publication *High Quality Care for All*, he defined clinical quality as *a combination of patient experience, patient safety and clinical effectiveness* (Department of Health 2008: 45). He also reinforced the need for greater integrated care facilities to be developed in communities to prevent people having to attend their local hospitals. In many places around the country, different integrated care projects were already being developed and alternative community-based facilities established, such as walk-in centres, healthy living centres and minor injury units to prevent people having to go to Accident and Emergency. In response to Lord Darzi's work, the Department of Health (2007b) insisted that each PCT should set up a 'polyclinic', often referred to as a Darzi Centre, in their areas. This directive took little or no account of local plans already being put in place and was often very unpopular, even if the underlying concept was supported.

By 2009, we were starting to see the development of more respectful relationships between commissioners and providers as the PCTs' abilities at commissioning started to mature and more Practice-based Commissioning Groups started to work more collaboratively with PCT management. Lord Darzi had also raised the importance of ensuring that services which are commissioned reflect people's life pathways from birth to death (Department of Health 2008). In a number of areas, this led to PCTs starting to change their approach to commissioning and to mixed commissioner/provider working groups being established to help develop integrated approaches to delivering children's services, support for long-term conditions or end-of-life care. Some PCTs, such as Great Yarmouth and Waveney and Norfolk, set up multi-professional programme boards based on these pathways, comprising both commissioners and providers, encouraging a greater partnership approach to redesigning services.

The challenge of enabling providers to earn an appropriate rate of return while being held to account for value for money and quality continued.

Then, we had an election.

TIPS FOR SUCCESS

In order to learn from past experience:

- *it is important to recognise that GP involvement in commissioning health services has existed in one form or other for over 20 years;*

- *multi-professional involvement in commissioning, especially involving allied health professionals, truly reflects the patient's experience;*

- *to commission or be commissioned effectively, commissioners and providers require knowledge of the system and practical skills.*

The new health environment

The Health and Social Care Act 2012 – a summary

The coalition government published its draft policy *Equity and Excellence: Liberating the NHS* in July 2010 (Department of Health 2010a). A lengthy period of consultation then took place when views were gathered from a wide range of different people using a variety of methods. There was considerable opposition from all quarters which has continued throughout, especially about the Any Qualified Provider proposals to enable any organisation to put itself forward as a potential competitor to traditional NHS provider organisations. The responses received formed the basis of the Health and Social Care Bill, which was debated at length through most of 2011 and the early part of 2012 in both Houses of Parliament as well as going through an extended committee stage.

As a result of the many negative responses to the Bill, the government decided to pause, appoint a Future Forum (Department of Health 2012b) led by Professor Steve Field, comprising a range of experts, and carry out a 'listening exercise' involving many people around the country, including NHS staff, patients and members of the public and others who have a stake in its future.

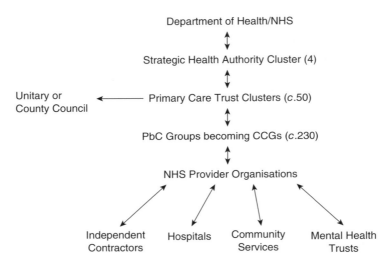

Figure 3.4 The NHS structure 2010–2012

This culminated in a revised Health and Social Care Act which finally received royal assent in April 2012.

While this was happening, the fact that the White Paper proposed abolishing both SHAs and PCTs inevitably led to senior people starting to look for other jobs. Also, the realisation of the extent of the economic recession led to the perceived levels of NHS management becoming the primary targets for budget cutting. This led to the number of SHAs being reduced from ten to four and the 152 PCTs being grouped together in 52 cluster arrangements (Figure 3.4).

Specifically, the Act did the following:

1. It separated out the NHS from the Department of Health to:

    (a) form an independent NHS Commissioning Board Authority (NHSCBA), with effect from October 2012, which is responsible for the NHS budget and for setting the framework of commissioning for NHS services in England. The NHSCBA, now called NHS England, is responsible for commissioning specialist services and also prison health, primary care (including GPs, dentists, optometrists and pharmacists, whose contracts are negotiated nationally) and health services for the armed forces.

    (b) leave the much smaller Department of Health to focus mainly on public health and prevention of ill health, through its agency, known as Public Health England.

2. It established that the Secretary of State is responsible for issuing an annual mandate for the NHS, setting out the government's priorities over the next three years, but refreshed each year.

3. The NHS Commissioning Board, now called NHS England, became responsible for establishing an infrastructure of regional and local offices probably working at the level of SHAs, i.e. South of England, London, Midlands and East, North of England and smaller local area offices. SHAs were abolished in April 2013. It is responsible for authorising CCGs and the Commissioning Support Organisations.

4. All GP practices are required to be members of their local CCG as a condition of their contract and the CCG must operate and be governed as a membership-led organisation. Its governing body comprises a minimum of elected GPs from the area, representatives of secondary care and nursing, lay representatives with special responsibility for governance and patient and public involvement.

5. Commissioning Support Organisations, based on a larger geographical area than PCTs, provide services to CCGs. These services typically cover data analysis, procurement, contract negotiation, management and monitoring. PCTs ceased to exist from 31 March 2013. In time, CCGs will be able to buy their support services in from other sectors.

6. There is to be much more emphasis on public involvement. The quote used is: 'no decision about me without me' at an individual patient level. At a local level, Healthwatch organisations replace the previous Local Involvement Networks, known as LINks, and have a seat on the local Health and Wellbeing Board. It is intended that local Healthwatch organisations will have greater national influence through a national coordinating body known as Healthwatch England which, in turn, now has a direct link into the Care Quality Commission.

7. The National Institute for Health and Clinical Excellence, responsible for developing best-practice pathways for patients, is now called the National Institute for Health and Care Excellence, reflecting the consistent drive towards greater health and social care integration.

8. Foundation Trusts continue but are now required to hold their board meetings in public. All Foundation Trusts are now able to generate private income equivalent to 49 per cent of their NHS income. There is also a new procedure which will allow poor-performing Foundation Trusts to fail. This is similar to the liquidation procedure for companies. Greater powers are to be given to Foundation Trust governors and members in future.

9. Monitor has an extended responsibility as economic regulator of the NHS and now incorporates the Competition and Co-operation Panel. A new special health authority, called the Trust Development Authority, now oversees the development of those NHS trusts that require more time to reach the standard required for Foundation Trust status.

10. Each high-level local authority, i.e. county council or unitary council, is now required to set up a Health and Wellbeing Board as a formal committee of the council, although it does not require full council approval for its decisions. It comprises, as a minimum, elected councillors, Healthwatch,

Director of Public Health, CCG Board GP representatives and the council directors responsible for adult social services and children and families. It is responsible for setting the overall Health and Wellbeing Strategy for local people, carrying out the Joint Strategic Needs Assessment and promoting greater integrated commissioning and integrated service delivery. It also has a role to play in advising NHS England on CCG authorisation and NHS England has a representative on each Health and Wellbeing Board.

11. A special authority called Health Education England is established to oversee a multi-professional approach to workforce planning and education to ensure the NHS has the necessary skills and expertise it needs for the twenty-first century. This is supported by provider-led Local Education and Training Boards which are required to provide the necessary service level perspective to ensure the quantity and quality of health professionals can meet the current and future needs of the system.

12. All parties are now required to operate in accordance with the NHS Constitution (see Appendix 2) which, in effect, represents a redefinition of the NHS values, suitable for a twenty-first-century world. In the 2012 Act, everyone has a duty to give regard to these values in the way in which they operate.

13. The NHS system will be judged much more on the basis of the outcomes it achieves rather than the inputs, thus changing the nature of monitoring and the focus of everyone's energy. There is now a National Outcomes Framework and commissioning at a local level will need to be more outcomes-focused.

From April 2013, the health economy should look as illustrated in Figure 3.5.

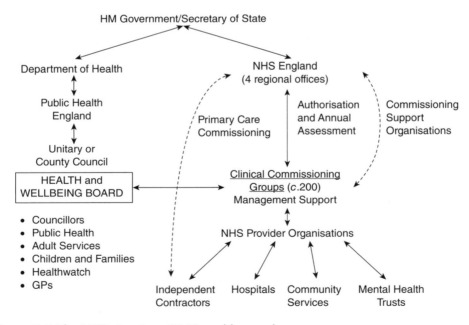

Figure 3.5 The NHS structure 2013 and beyond

How were the Clinical Commissioning Groups formed?

It is important to remember that PCTs were abolished on 31 March 2013. Before then, officially 80 per cent of NHS funds were still the responsibility of the 152 PCTs. For reasons of budget and pragmatism, these formed into approximately 50 PCT clusters in 2010. SHAs and PCTs were jointly responsible for managing the transition to CCGs while delivering savings of an estimated £20bn under the Quality, Innovation, Productivity and Prevention (QIPP) agenda at the same time as they had to plan their own demise by April 2013.

Most CCGs have emerged from the Practice-based Commissioning Groups which had been developed by the last administration. In a number of cases, these had already started to mature into effective GP-led organisations, combining commissioning and development of services, and had started to accept increasing levels of responsibility from the PCTs. Often they had set themselves up as community interest companies or social enterprises, improving current services and developing new ones, in partnership with PCT commissioners and colleagues in provider organisations. Throughout this period, the PCT remained the legally accountable body responsible for the contracts.

The Health and Social Care Act 2012 (Department of Health 2012c) changed this. It converted the situation so that managers are no longer on top, with doctors and nurses on tap, but the other way around (www.yhcpc.nhs.uk). The original White Paper panicked many GPs into believing that they would have to do the commissioning of all services, while still carrying on with their busy day jobs. The intent, in fact, is that clinicians lead the strategy of what needs to be commissioned and then delegate the actual job of commissioning to managers who either work directly for them in the CCGs or indirectly for them but employed by the emerging Commissioning Support Organisations.

As with GP fundholding, while many clinicians do not support the new approach and the need for legislation, many can understand the potential power which the new arrangements gives to primary care clinicians to achieve the changes many have wanted to make for years. While the media continued to carry stories about the opposition, 257 Pathfinder CCGs had signed up with the Department of Health by July 2011 (Department of Health 2011), long before the legislation was passed.

At a local level, many of the Practice-based Commissioning Groups that had set up formal companies had to disestablish them and agree to become subcommittees of the existing PCTs. In conjunction with the Local Medical Committees, with advice from the British Medical Association, local GPs elected their representatives on to a Transitional Board of a Pathfinder or shadow CCG and agreed allowances/release of time from their practices to carry out their new roles.

The newly elected Transitional GP Boards each appointed a chair from amongst its number. These boards often included nurses, practice managers, allied health professionals, representatives of secondary care and lay representatives and employed a small management team to support them. Most shadow CCGs started to engage with their local PCT with a view to understanding better the responsibilities they would have by April 2013, getting involved with 'live' commissioning with providers. To differing extents, PCT staff were often transferred or aligned to them.

GP members of CCG governing bodies were nominated to represent the CCG's interests on the shadow Health and Wellbeing Boards which started to be developed by their local county or unitary councils, working alongside locally elected councillors and directors of social care budgets and public health. Together they started to work on the Joint Strategic Needs Assessment for their local population and to agree priority issues which need to be worked on, such as improving access, reducing inequality, increasing self-care and more integrated community-based care.

An evolving membership organisation

NHS England, led currently by Sir David Nicholson, has already made it very clear that the new CCGs, which are statutory bodies in their own right following authorisation, will be very different organisations from PCTs. In the guidance issued (NHS Commissioning Board 2012: 3) for CCG authorisation, it was formally acknowledged that they will need time to mature.

> *CCG authorisation recognises that CCGs are new, clinically-led organisations coming into being for the first time. While aspiring CCGs are already showing commitment to being as good as they can possibly be, the full potential of clinical leadership of commissioning will emerge over time through learning from innovation and experience. At the same time, authorisation must ensure CCGs meet safe thresholds to assume their full statutory responsibilities. For this reason, authorisation of CCGs is designed as a maturity model in which thresholds of authorisation are set in the context of a longer term vision drawn from what aspiring CCGs are already striving to deliver. Therefore authorisation should not be seen as an end in itself, but as a first step on a journey towards continuous improvement.*

(NHS Commissioning Board 2012: 3)

One of the main difficulties is that most CCGs have had to start organising themselves without knowing the regulations which would describe exactly how the legislation would be enacted. For example, most had Transitional Boards already, including elected GPs. Due to the regulations, all of them have had to carry out another set of elections and ensure that their member practices collectively wish to become a CCG. Additional changes have had to be made to comply with the rules on appointing a secondary care clinician and a registered nurse, from outside the area, as well as the lay representatives leading on public involvement and governance.

It is likely that by now all GP practices realise that membership of their local CCG will be a condition of their own contract to practise in the NHS. Every member practice must appoint a clinician to act on their behalf. Such representatives will form the CCG Council of Members and be expected to be the 'backbone' of the CCG's distributed leadership (NHS Commissioning Board 2012: 8) in shaping the future provision of healthcare to ensure it reflects what their patients and communities need.

The member practices will have been involved already in developing a constitution for their CCG which sets out how the CCG operates and is governed. This has to cover issues such as:

- the membership, roles, tenure and size of the CCG Board and how they are appointed/elected;
- how decisions are made and the relative roles and responsibilities of the CCG governing body and its member practices;
- how information is communicated and how consultation is carried out;
- what structures support the governance of the CCG, including subcommittees of the governing body and possibly locality structures for member practices.

The constitution must also cover potential contentious issues such as:

- how to handle conflicts of interest;
- how to handle practices that do not comply with the constitution;
- how to manage situations where practices are poorly performing.

Although a formal legal document, it is important that everyone is clear about what the respective roles and responsibilities of the member practices and their elected/appointed governing body are. For many, this means taking time to get the basics right, but the early investment should produce real benefits, not least a higher level of trust, later on.

The journey to authorisation

From April 2013, NHS England (previously the NHSCBA) has been responsible for all the NHS funds and commissioning of services and will only delegate commissioning responsibilities to CCGs if they are sufficiently competent. NHS England started operating in shadow form in April 2012 and has been officially in place since October 2012. The authorisation process for CCGs officially began in July 2012, with further waves in September, October and November 2012, with a view to having all CCGs authorised by April 2013.

What did the authorisation process comprise?

Officially, the authorisation process was designed to test six key domains:

1. a strong clinical and professional focus which brings real added value;

2. meaningful engagement with patients, carers and their communities;

3. clear and credible plans which continue to meet the QIPP challenge within financial resources;

4. proper constitutional and governance arrangements, with the capacity and capability to deliver all their duties and responsibilities, including financial control as well as effectively commission all the services for which they are responsible;

5. collaborative arrangements for commissioning with other CCGs, local authorities and NHS England as well as the appropriate external commissioning support;

6. great leaders who individually and collectively can make a real difference.

Each of these six domains is backed up by a number of competence areas, as set out in Table 3.1.

In summary, this may be a simpler way of remembering what is required.

There were three key people:

1. the CCG chair – this could either be a lay representative or, more often, a GP who has been elected by the member practices and appointed by their governing body colleagues;

2. the accountable officer – in effect the key executive leader who will work full-time for the CCG. The accountable officer may or may not be a clinician;

3. the chief finance officer, responsible for ensuring the CCG is financially sound.

Anyone in these posts or who wished to be a candidate for one of these positions had to have attended a nationally organised development centre which tested their levels of competency for the roles through a number of scenarios and role play and well as psychometric tests. There are three possible outcomes: the individual is 'ready to appoint'; he or she has some development needs; or he or she is 'not ready to appoint'. Whatever the outcome, NHS England was required to ratify the appointment of the accountable officer and chief finance officer.

There were three stages of the authorisation process: pre-application, application and decision.

1. The pre-application stage consisted of:

- a CCG profile prepared by NHS England;

- a report from the local SHA (when they existed) about the CCG's progress to date;

- a 360-degree web-based stakeholder survey which was carried out with 40–45 of the CCG's stakeholders to seek their opinion on the CCG's competence. These stakeholders included patient and public groups such as Healthwatch, the member practices, council and neighbouring CCG co-commissioners and provider organisations, such as the local hospital, community services and mental health trusts. The results of the survey were sent to the CCG for their comments.

Table 3.1 Clinical Commissioning Group (CCG) authorisation: six domains

A strong clinical and multi-professional focus which brings real added value	A great CCG will have a clinical focus perspective threaded through everything it does, resulting in having quality at its heart, and a real focus on outcomes. It will have significant engagement from its constituent practices as well as widespread involvement of all other clinical colleagues, clinicians providing health services locally, including secondary care, community and mental health, those providing services to people with learning disabilities, public health experts, as well as social care colleagues. It will communicate a clear vision of the improvements it is seeking to make in the health of the locality, including population health.
Meaningful engagement with patients, carers and their communities	CCGs need to be able to show they will ensure inclusion of patients, carers, public, communities of interest and geography, Health and Wellbeing Boards and local authorities. They should include mechanisms for gaining a broad range of views, then analysing and acting on these. It should be evident how the views of individual patients are translated into commissioning decisions and how the voice of each practice population will be sought and acted on. CCGs need to promote shared decision making with patients, about their care.
Clear and credible plans which continue to deliver the Quality, Innovation, Productivity and Prevention (QIPP) challenge within financial resources, in line with national requirements (including excellent outcomes), and local Joint Health and Wellbeing Strategies	CCGs should have a credible plan for how they will continue to deliver the local QIPP challenge for their health system, and meet the NHS Constitution requirements. These plans will set out how the CCG will take responsibility for service transformation that will improve outcomes, quality and productivity, whilst reducing unwarranted variation and tackling inequalities, within their financial allocation. They need a track record of delivery and progress against these plans, within whole-system working, and contracts in place to ensure future delivery. CCGs will need to demonstrate how they will exercise important functions, such as the need to promote research.
Proper constitutional and governance arrangements, with the capacity and capability to deliver all their duties and responsibilities, including financial control, as well as effectively commission all the services for which they are responsible	CCGs need the capacity and capability to carry out their corporate and commissioning responsibilities. This means they must be properly constituted with all the right governance arrangements. They must be able to deliver all their statutory functions, strategic oversight, financial control and probity, as well as driving quality, encouraging innovation and managing risk. They must be committed to, and capable of, delivering on important agendas included in the NHS Constitution, such as equality and diversity, safeguarding and choice. They must have appropriate arrangements for day-to-day business, e.g. communications. They must also have all the process in place to commission effectively each and every one of those services for which they are responsible, from the early health needs assessment through service design, planning and reconfiguration to procurement, contract monitoring and quality control.

(Continued)

Table 3.1 (Continued)

Collaborative arrangements for commissioning with other CCGs, local authorities and NHS England as well as appropriate external commissioning support	CCGs need robust arrangements for working with other CCGs in order to commission key services across wider geographies and play their part in major service reconfiguration. They also need strong shared leadership with local authorities to develop Joint Health and Wellbeing Strategies, and strong arrangements for joint commissioning with local authorities to commission services where integration of health and social care is vital and the ability to secure expert public health advice when this is needed. They also need to have credible commissioning support arrangements in place to ensure robust commissioning and economies of scale. They need to be able to support NHS England in its role of commissioner of primary care and work with the Board as a partner to integrate commissioning where appropriate.
Great leaders who individually and collectively can make a real difference	Together, CCG leaders must be able to lead health commissioning for their population and drive transformational change to deliver improved outcomes. These leaders need to demonstrate their commitment to, and understanding of, partnership working in line with such senior public roles, as well as the necessary skill set to take an oversight of public services. They need individual clinical leaders who can drive change, and a culture which distributes leadership throughout the organisation. The accountable officer needs to be capable of steering such a significant organisation and the chief finance officer must be both fully qualified and have sufficient experience. All those on the governing body will need to have the right skills.

2. The application stage consisted of:

- the submission of a detailed application form, which had to include certification by the chair of the CCG governing body and accountable officer that they were compliant with the six domains. Their application form had to be supported by written evidence, as set out in Table 3.2.

The CCGs were required to demonstrate real improvements for local people and to categorise these according to specific groups within the population. These were listed as:

- mothers and newborns;
- people who need support for mental health;
- people with learning disabilities;
- people who need emergency and urgent care;
- people who need routine operations;
- people with long-term conditions;
- people with continuing healthcare needs;
- people who need support at the end of their lives.

Table 3.2 Supporting information required for Clinical Commissioning Group (CCG) authorisation

- CCG strategic plan
- Constitution
- Joint Strategic Needs Assessment (JSNA)
- Health and Wellbeing Strategy (draft)
- Future commissioning intentions
- Organisational structure
- Minutes of meetings/subcommittees
- Contracts with providers
- Contract with commissioning support organisation
- Letter of support for chair signed by all practices
- Organisational development plan to show how CCG's capacity is being developed
- Case studies

The documentation was checked against the self-certification and any gaps identified formed the basis of the Key Lines of Enquiry, which were pursued in a site visit. Examples of these might have included the level of practice engagement or public engagement or assessment of service quality:

- the CCG's response to the stakeholder survey;
- a site visit by a team comprising representatives from NHS England and experts in commissioning and finance and possibly additional experts from public health and local government.

The results of this stage were then presented internally to a panel of NHS England who made the final decision. There was no appeal and if the CCG was found to have knowingly falsified any of its application, the application would have been automatically disqualified.

3. The process and final decision by NHS England has tended to reflect the fact that the CCGs will continue to mature and develop so they have all received recommended areas for further improvement, even if they were successful. The decisions took the form of:

    (a) *full authorisation*, in which case the CCG officially took over responsibility for the commissioning budget from the PCT with effect from 1 April 2013;

    (b) *conditional authorisation* – conditions may be 'major' or 'minor', but there would be some restriction on what the CCG can do to be able to commission and a rectification plan outlining what needs to be done and an agreed timescale for compliance;

(c) *established but not authorised*, in which case the CCG would be issued a more extensive rectification plan with an agreed timescale for compliance. Arrangements will be agreed for the commissioning responsibility for that area to be allocated either to a neighbouring CCG which has been fully authorised or responsibility will be retained by NHS England.

Thereafter, the CCGs and their development plans will be reviewed annually by NHS England to ensure they are maintaining the necessary standards.

CASE STUDY 3.1

Ipswich and East Suffolk Clinical Commissioning Group (CCG)

The three Practice-based Commissioning groups in East Suffolk resolved shortly after the White Paper was published in July 2010 to operate as a single CCG. Together with colleagues in Ipswich CCG, they then invested in blocks of time to meet together to understand fully the CCG concept, the way the NHS and social care systems worked and the real challenges. Without shying away from the considerable challenges in their health economy, they maintained a balanced focus on the opportunities which CCG status offered for them to make real improvement in services as well.

It soon became clear that the two groups – Ipswich and East Suffolk – shared similar ambitions and, actively involving their member practices, decided to merge.

The merger also gave them a stronger negotiating position with their large main providers, all of whom were facing considerable service quality and financial pressures.

The new CCG came together quickly and, as a priority, set up workshops with their counterpart clinical and executive leaders in the acute and mental health providers. The aim of these was to discuss and share their strategic vision – not to negotiate. These events resulted in agreement about ongoing clinician-to-clinician reviews of provider performance alongside contract review meetings; agreement on joint plans for improving provider performance; as well as a commitment to develop joint leadership development arrangements so that future generations of primary and secondary care clinicians would understand one another's perspectives better.

They have carried out extensive consultation on their plans with local patients and the public, as well as with a wide range of special interest groups, and have built up a regular programme of communication and consultation. They have also invested time and effort in building strong links with the county council.

Throughout the last two years, the CCG has worked hard to maintain strong support from its member practices. Well over 20 GPs applied for the few positions on the governing body and remain actively involved as clinical leads. They have also put energy into the fundamental challenge of integrating service delivery by running local workshops for frontline staff from practices, community mental health, community services and social care to devise better ways of caring for patients.

Perhaps one of the ways they have managed to sustain their energy and commitment is by building an extensive track record by simply 'just getting on with service improvement'.

TIPS FOR SUCCESS

In order for CCGs to be fully effective:

- investment in leadership development pays off in the short term and the long term;

- relationships with all stakeholders must be nurtured and given high priority;

- nurture your member practices – keep them informed and involved with what you do;

- keep your focus on your purpose – improving services and care for patients.

The challenges of commissioning in this sector

Although there are already so many people who are predicting that the new system will fail, GP commissioning has had a very long gestation period. To become a doctor you have to be intelligent. To run a successful business, such as a large GP practice, you have to know how to manage resources to ensure supply meets demand. So what positive changes could we look forward to?

Focusing on what is important rather than what is measured

While there was a real risk that the authorisation process could take over the day-to-day lives of anyone involved with a CCG, in the same way as the Foundation Trust authorisation process completely takes over the lives of its leadership teams, there is evidence that most CCGs are determined to focus on their fundamental purpose – to improve patient care.

GPs are used to being their own masters and many of them are accustomed to running medium-sized businesses. Politically, they have demonstrated that they have little patience with civil servants or unnecessary bureaucracy. Practice managers are highly respected by GPs because of their business acumen and their ability to implement decisions quickly. It remains to be seen how GPs will behave in respect to slow decision-making processes and the new national and regional structures of NHS England, especially if the latter forget that they are supposed to behave differently too!

There are already signs that many are structuring themselves in such a way as to 'feed' the NHS 'beast' but ensuring that the GPs, in particular, spend most of their time doing what they should be best at, which is ensuring and assuring that services for patients are the best they can be.

What commissioner–provider split?

There is also evidence that GPs are realising that there is one critical success factor which cannot be ignored: the need to break down the barriers between primary and secondary care and to end the adversarial behaviour and lack of mutual respect which are too often evident between commissioners and providers.

CCGs, such as Ipswich and East Suffolk, have made joint workshops between themselves and their main hospital and mental health providers a priority. This has enabled both parties, with more clinicians than managers in the same room, to get to know one another as professional people, realise they want the same outcomes and then to start working together for the benefit of their patients.

Health and Wellbeing Boards

This concept, which brings together as equals those who have the political mandate, i.e. councillors, those who have the information, i.e. public health, those who have the budgets, i.e. council directors and GP commissioners with the local people, i.e. Healthwatch, is truly revolutionary. The Health and Wellbeing Board must not be allowed to become a 'talking shop'. Instead, like Kensington and Chelsea and Harrow, it must become a 'meeting of minds': a place where fundamental challenges are worked through and resolved or, at least, contained; challenges such as real integration of frontline health and social care staff are enabled; where resources are shared to ensure the public take more responsibility for their own health and care but know where to go if they need help; and where all the key agencies can be brought together to focus on the 'troubled families' who use a disproportionate share of precious public funds. In other words, they should focus on health and wellbeing and focus on those 'wicked issues' which they are the ideal group to solve.

Courage to tackle the 'elephant in the room'

At a local level, GPs are fast realising the fundamental problem: even with the doubling of NHS funds which took place during the Labour government, we can never meet the continually growing demands from a continually growing population who have grown to assume that they can have any and every treatment free on the 'National Health'.

If GPs can collaborate effectively with one another and the other health professionals in their community, they could collaborate nationally as well and help our society redefine the NHS for the twenty-first century. Which services should be free at the point of delivery and which should be funded by other means? What are the respective responsibilities of the individual citizen, families, communities and the state?

This might help us to have exactly the same vital debate about social care.

Chapter 4
Commissioning in adult social care

CHAPTER OBJECTIVES

By the end of this chapter you should be able to:

- understand the challenges and opportunities associated with commissioning adult social care;
- appreciate how adult social care is developing and how this will impact on commissioning;
- understand the emerging role of local authorities.

The development of commissioning in adult social care

Whilst commissioning for adult social care is similar in many respects to that found in other sectors, it differs in that it operates at more than one level. The Care Services Improvement Partnership (2006: 2) identifies a dual emphasis, firstly micro-commissioning in respect of individuals and secondly, at a strategic level, shaping the local care market.

Commissioning, in the context of personalisation, has been defined as *working together with citizens and providers to support individuals to translate their aspirations into timely and quality services which meet their needs, enable choice and control, are cost effective and support the whole community* (In Control 2009: 1). In Control outlines three levels of commissioning: strategic, operational and citizen (In Control 2009: 2). Strategic commissioning includes area-wide and regional-level commissioning whilst operational commissioning focuses on making care services work in a locality and supporting citizens to commission. Citizen-level commissioning refers to citizens who direct their own care and support.

The emerging practice of commissioning for adult social care reflects:

- the general environmental factors and actions of Conservative, Labour and coalition governments, outlined in Chapter 2 and illustrated in Figure 4.1. This sector has also experienced the move towards greater private sector

involvement and a more commercial paradigm, pressure to improve performance and collaborate and encouragement of greater citizen involvement; and

- sector-specific sociological and economic environmental factors and government action.

Sociological and economic environmental factors

For adult social care and health, sociological and economic factors combine to
create a 'time bomb' caused by a combination of projected significant increases
in demand and tight public finances.

The UK population is growing and ageing at the same time. In 2010, the UK population was 62.3 million, a figure that is projected to rise to 67.2 million by 2020
and 73.2 million by 2035 (ONS 2010a). The number of UK citizens aged over 85
doubled to 1.4 million between 1985 and 2010 and is projected to rise to 3.5
million by 2035 (ONS 2012).

Males born in 1911 were expected to live to 49.4 years of age and females to 53.1
years. By 1951 these ages had risen to 65.6 and 70.4 years and by 2010 to 78.5
and 82.4 years for males and females respectively.

In 2006, life expectancy for those aged 65 was a further 17.2 years for men and a further 19.9 for women, up from 13 years (men) and 16.9 years (women) in 1981. Within

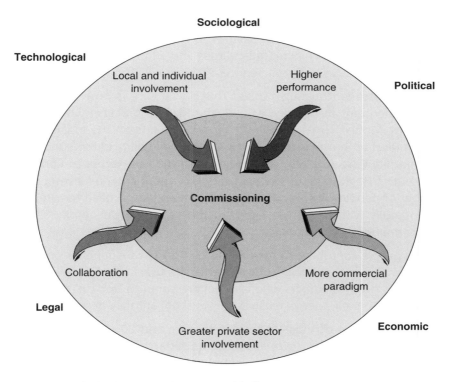

Figure 4.1 Commissioning – environmental influences

this expectancy, men can expect 12.9 years of good or fairly good health and women 14.5 years (2006). On average, men can expect to have more significant health and social care needs for 4.3 years and women for 5.4 years (ONS 2010b: 3–5).

People are living longer than in previous generations due to better standards of living and higher standards of healthcare. With longevity comes age-related conditions such as dementia; an increasing number of older people will develop a complex mix of physical, mental health and social care needs which require very high levels of support.

Approximately 1.5 million people receive care in England; of these, 380,000 people are in residential settings (Department of Health 2012a: 7). Adult social care commissioned by local authorities is funded by a mix of central government grant, council tax, fees and charges. The total amount spent on social care is determined each year by local authority elected members and there is competition for resources with children's services, highways, trading standards and other services. This is a difficult problem at the best of times, even more so with rising demand and pressure and reductions in local authority total spending.

Budgeted local authority revenue spending in 2012–2013 was £98.4bn, down from £104.3bn in 2010–2011. Adult social care is expected to account for 12.9 per cent of total spending (£14.7bn) in 2012–2013, down 1.1 per cent on the previous year (Department for Communities and Local Government 2012). A survey conducted by the Association of Directors of Social Services in April/May 2012 revealed that: *Directors of adult social services in England are in the process of taking £890 million out of the nation's total social care budget between April this year [2012] and March 2013.* Savings include £688m from service redesign and efficiency, £77m from increased charges and £113m from service reductions (Association of Directors of Social Services 2012a).

There is a widespread mistaken belief that social care is both widely available and free at the point of delivery, as with the NHS. In practice, whether a person receives state-funded social care and support depends on the individual level of need. Each local authority is required to draw up eligibility criteria under the NHS and Community Care Act 1990 and in line with the Fair Access to Care guidance (Department of Health 2003). The application of these criteria leaves a considerable number of people with significant but less than critical need to care for themselves, hopefully with help from family members, friends, neighbours, voluntary or other community organisations.

How much people contribute to the cost of their social care depends on their financial resources. This is a particular concern for service users who fear selling their own homes and for family members who can feel pressured to 'top up' financial contributions to ensure their relative receives the level of care they desire.

Currently 65 per cent of those in residential care and 80 per cent of those who receive care at home are state-supported (Department of Health 2012a: 8). Significant self-funding of social care coupled with informal care by an estimated five million family members, friends and neighbours as well as by clubs, community organisations and charities means that even now the public purse does not meet the full cost of care. These forms of care will need to make an even bigger contribution in future.

Government actions

Arguably, the most significant influences on social care are political. Since the 1946 National Assistance Act which created the NHS and separated health and social care, many changes have been made in pursuit of a system that is economic, efficient and effective. These changes also reflect attempts by successive governments to cope with the implications of sociological trends, economic conditions, technological developments and other environmental influences.

Actions of the current coalition government are informed by the 2010 document *A Vision for Adult Social Care – Capable Communities and Active Citizens* (Department of Health 2010d: 4), which promotes the idea that we should *strengthen communities, while changing the role and our relationship with the state*. The vision expressed a wish to make *services more personalised, more preventative and more focused on delivering the best outcomes for those that use them* (Department of Health 2010d: 6). It also articulated the values of freedom, fairness and responsibility. Freedom reflects a wish to see a *real shift of power from the state to people and communities* (Department of Health 2010d: 4) with users free to choose services from a *vibrant plural market* and professionals free from local authority procedures (Department of Health 2010d: 4). Fairness concerns how care is paid for and how carers are supported and paid. Responsibility signals a shift towards personal and community responsibility. The vision for adult social care is built on principles that should lead to a care system where:

- individuals are independent and exercise control;
- care and support need is met by a healthy market comprising high-quality, highly productive providers working in collaboration;
- the whole care workforce provide care and support imaginatively, allowing freedom whilst ensuring sensible safeguards.

Actions of successive governments with regard to adult social care fall within three themes:

1. shifting the emphasis of care from residential to community care and from provision to prevention;

2. a drive to personalisation and greater client involvement;

3. encouragement for agencies to collaborate.

The shift from residential to community care and from provision to prevention

The shift from residential to community care was signalled as long ago as the 1950s when there was concern regarding the number of people with mental illness or mental disability in residential care. The provisions of the Health Service and Public Health Act 1968, the Chronically Sick and Disabled Act 1971, the introduction of Invalidity Benefit in 1971 and Invalidity Pensions and Invalid Care Allowances in 1975 were all part of a shift towards community provision, increasing local authority powers to provide a range of community-based services and providing financial support for clients and, in certain situations, for care assistants. The NHS and Community Care Act 1990 required local authorities to promote the independent sector, inspect services, establish complaints procedures and prepare Community Care Plans.

The focus for state care and resource allocation has traditionally been frail older people and those requiring acute care, as shown at the apex of a triangle of care in Figure 4.2 where relatively few people with significant need account for a high proportion of spending (Association of Directors of Social Services 2003: 9).

The shift in emphasis from treatment and care to prevention and wellbeing is more recent and recognises that early support for people with moderate or low-level need can prevent, minimise and delay the need for more intensive care. Avoiding future cost is a somewhat limited ambition and there is growing recognition that investing in community development and prevention should lead to more people having a better quality of life for longer, delaying the point at which they would otherwise need more intensive care.

In 2003, the Association of Directors of Social Services (2003: 9) suggested that the triangle of care be inverted so that community strategy and preventive policies are at the top and therefore receive greater attention and investment. This is illustrated in Figure 4.3. The Association of Directors of Social Care recognised that the traditional view of prevention needed to evolve from *services which prevent or delay the need for more costly intensive services* to *strategies and approaches that promote the quality of life of older people and their engagement in the community* (Association of Directors of Social Care 2012b: 10).

Figure 4.2 Triangle of care

Figure 4.3 Inverted triangle of care

For this second shift to occur, communities need to assume collective responsibility for wellbeing, agencies need to collaborate to ensure services are available to support people and professionals need to become enablers.

However logical investing in prevention to avoid future spending on crisis care and improve quality of life might be, achieving this in practice is difficult. A lack of evidence of the longer-term financial benefit of prevention, high crisis demand from current service users, significant time delays before the benefits of prevention spending are realised and the electoral cycle combine to focus attention and resources on crisis. This is further exacerbated by financial arrangements that mean that, whilst prevention tends to be funded from local authority budgets, financial benefits largely accrue to health organisations. However, thinking is changing and there is a growing interest in outcomes, performance measurement and understanding social return on investment. The Partnerships for Older People Projects in 2010 (Personal Social Services Research Unit 2010) concluded that measures such as fitting grab rails, providing assistive technology, running specialist falls programmes and hospital discharge services result in fewer

Table 4.1 Stages of care

Stages of care	Aim	Likely action
Living well	Prevent care needs and ensure better connections to people around the individual	Provision of information and advice
Low-level needs	Maintain independence and avoid a crisis	Support within communities, better housing options and improved support for carers
Crisis	Regain independence and avoid long-term care	Crisis support and reablement

overnight hospital stays, lower attendance at Accident and Emergency departments and reduced demand on GP services. The report concluded that, in addition to improving service users' quality of life, every £1 spent on older preventive social care services saved £1.20 in spending on emergency beds.

The White Paper *Caring for Our Future: Reforming Care and Support* sets out a new vision for a reformed care and support system, identifying three stages that are similar to those in the inverted pyramid of care (Department of Health 2012a: 8). Table 4.1 explains for each stage the aim and actions that might be involved.

TIPS FOR SUCCESS

Significant pressure on resources has traditionally been a barrier to investing in prevention, even more so with wellbeing. At the heart of this problem, however, is the traditional assumption that prevention or wellbeing work requires direct state provision, or at least state funding, normally by one agency. In order to be successful in future:

- *commissioners need to plan on the basis of community-wide public funds, not just the money that is available to a single agency;*
- *other formal and informal resources across the community must be taken into account when planning;*
- *public sector use of resources needs to be considered as an investment rather than as spending;*
- *a more developed sense of the value of different forms of support, activities and intervention is required – this requires a commitment to developing measures of social return on investment;*
- *more time needs to be spent considering how self-care and other forms of informal care can be stimulated.*

Drive to personalisation and greater client involvement

In recent years, there has been an emphasis on service users and their carers being given greater choice and control over the services they receive. Within reason, this enables individuals to tailor their package so that it reflects their prioritised needs. Local authorities have been challenged to give clients greater choice and control through mechanisms such as:

- direct payments, where recipients are given the money to employ people or commission services to meet their eligible needs;
- personal budgets, where funding is allocated to users. This allocation may be taken as a part or full direct payment or users can elect for councils to commission services on their behalf;
- individual service funds, where a personal budget is held by a care provider with the user free to choose how to spend some or all of it.

Take-up of personal budgets has increased from 93,000 in 2008–2009, to 432,349 in 2011–2012. In 2011–2012 alone there has been a 40 per cent increase and the value of personal budgets now stands at £2.6bn. Of those eligible, 52.8 per cent use personal budgets to arrange their care. There is, however, a marked variation in take-up between authorities.

The drive to personalisation continues. The coalition government is committed to giving people and their carers greater control, enabling better community-based provision and incentivising preventive action (Department of Health 2010d: 6). The 2010 spending review included a commitment to personal budgets and local authorities were challenged to *provide personal budgets, preferably as direct payments to everyone eligible within the next two years* (Department of Health 2010d: 4).

The White Paper *Caring for Our Future* stated that the *shift to a person-centred system is at the heart of our draft Care and Support Bill* (Department of Health 2012a: 20).

Encouragement to collaborate

In recent years, there have been many attempts to join up health and social care, thereby rectifying some of the problems caused by the 1946 National Assistance Act. This separated older and disabled people into those with health needs that would typically be met through stays in hospitals, and those requiring social care, typically met in local authority residential homes. In practice, many older and disabled people have a complex combination of needs and distinguishing between those that are health and social care in nature can be artificial and arbitrary and make effective care planning, management and delivery difficult. More generally, the interest in pooling resources to tackle 'wicked issues' is prompting collaboration. If the full benefits of commissioning, in general, and wellbeing investment, in particular, are to be realised, there needs to be a 'whole-community' approach with costs and benefits being seen to accrue to the community rather than the agencies within it.

Attempts to encourage joint working, partnerships and collaboration regarding adult social care include:

- the 1973 National Health Service Reorganisation Act which established joint consultative committees;

- the 1999 Health Act, which introduced new flexibilities such as pooled budgeting, lead commissioning and integrated provision;

- the development of intermediate care to facilitate the move from hospital to home following the national beds inquiry in 2000;

- the 2003 Community Care (Delayed Discharges etc.) Act which made local authorities financially responsible if they did not put in place services that allowed for patients to be discharged from hospital;

- the formation of Local Strategic Partnerships, Health and Wellbeing and other partnerships from 2000 onwards;

- the Local Government Act 2000 duty on local authorities to prepare Community Strategies;
- the Health and Social Care Act in 2012 which placed Health and Wellbeing Boards at the heart of the transformation of health and care. These boards will comprise leaders from across the community that will tackle a range of responsibilities, including the preparation of Joint Strategic Needs Assessments and Joint Health and Wellbeing Strategies.

Successful collaboration in adult social care requires effective relationships that extend beyond health and local authorities responsible for social care. The real benefits of commissioning will be seen only when collaboration exists between:

- social care and healthcare commissioners, housing services, environmental services, police, highways, public transport planners and a range of other public organisations;
- commissioners and formal care providers, e.g. home care and residential care organisations;
- formal care providers to ensure service integration;
- formal and informal care providers, including families, friends, neighbours and peers;
- commissioners, care providers and individuals seeking care;
- commissioners, providers, individuals seeking care and other citizens.

Collaboration across the whole community requires decentralisation and for localities to take back control. This is recognised by the Cameron administration. In a press release dated 6 April 2012 announcing the coming into effect of measures contained in the Localism Act 2011, Decentralisation Minister Greg Clark said:

> *Today is a major turning point in the balance of power in this country as new rights and freedoms for communities to take back control come into force. The historic Localism Act is beginning to reverse more than 100 years of centralisation, returning power back to citizens, communities and local groups to manage their own affairs free from Whitehall interference.*

These powerful reforms are the next step in breaking up the monopoly of Whitehall over public services, giving local people with good ideas the right to do things differently.

In July 2010, the Right Hon. Greg Clark stated that the Big Society consisted of three strands:

> *Firstly, public sector reform. Secondly, community empowerment. And thirdly, philanthropic action. Though these strands are intertwined, they are also distinct. The first is about what the state can do for us. The second is about what we can do for ourselves. And the third is about what we can do for others. All three are essential to the Big Society.*

(Clark 2010)

These comments were based on a speech made a week earlier in Liverpool by David Cameron (British Political Speeches 2010).

Commissioning offers a framework within which everyone can engage in conversation that leads to actions which:

- result in better outcomes for individuals and the community;

- stimulate innovation relating to wellbeing, prevention and provision;

- improve economy and efficiency;

- enable effective whole-system responses to 'wicked problems';

- result in behaviour change;

- redraw responsibilities and involvement in care by all stakeholders.

A developing view of adult social care

Traditionally, older people's care is primarily associated with residential or home care provided by professional staff 'caring' for those with social care needs. This is changing, as indicated in the 2012 White Paper *Caring for Our Future: Reforming Care and Support,* which explains that:

> care and support enable people to do the everyday things that most of us take for granted: things like getting out of bed, dressed and into work; cooking meals; seeing friends; caring for our families; and being part of our communities. It might include emotional support at a time of difficulty or stress, or helping people who are caring for a family member or friend. It can mean support from community groups and networks, for example, giving others a lift to a social event. It might also include state-funded support, such as information and advice, support for carers, housing support, disability benefits and adult social care.

> (Department of Health 2012a: 13)

This covers a wide range of people, in terms of their age, whether they are in employment or not and whether the need is permanent or temporary. This definition recognises practical and financial care and support offered by families, friends, community groups and state support.

However, an even wider definition of care and support is possible – one that recognises five main forms of care, as illustrated in Figure 4.4.

- Self-care – those actions people can take to look after themselves, e.g. personal care, cooking, gardening, car maintenance, cleaning. Self-care helps maintain independence and because individuals remain in their homes friends and neighbours are better able to continue to provide support. This form of care incurs minimal cost for the Exchequer.

- Family care – typically, help with physical tasks, assistance with managing their affairs and simply 'being there'. This support helps individuals remain in their homes and community and where offered sensitively helps them to retain choice and control. Traditionally this form of care is provided at minimal cost to the Exchequer.

- Friends and neighbours – help with physical tasks, regular contact and conversation and generally looking out for each other. This has similar benefit to care provided by family members but, as it tends to be more constant, can reduce social isolation and may involve reciprocal support with peers. This form of care also involves minimal cost to the Exchequer.

- Not-for-profit organisations – a wide variety of services offered nationally, regionally or locally by charities, faith and community groups. These organisations provide services such as hospital transport, lunch clubs, evening companionship and generally help 'join up' other forms of care. This care is often quite informal in nature and involves little cost to the Exchequer.

- Commercial providers – a very wide range of services are available from companies, self-employed individuals, Foundation Trusts and provider units within public organisations. Services offered include those traditionally associated with social care, including home care, residential and day centres. Beyond this are services such as gardening, car and house maintenance, and taxis. Traditionally, this second group of services tends to be self-funded.

With respect to older people, the practice of recognising care and support when an arbitrary age is reached or threshold of need exceeded limits thinking and overemphasises formal care and the role of the state. It is estimated that *seventy-six per cent of people will need care and support at some point in*

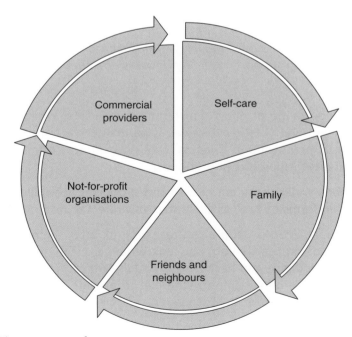

Figure 4.4 Five sources of care

later life (Department of Health 2012a: 13). Viewing care and support during the whole life of a person breaks down conventional silos within adult social care and paves the way for innovative, integrated responses to meeting need. Furthermore, adult social care should not be seen as separate from that for children and young people. There is a need for an organic and dynamic relationship between commissioning plans across the age range. It is *particularly important that plans for adults have such a relationship with the Children and Young People's Plan, and that this relationship is an active and ongoing one that extends into the operational delivery phase* (In Control 2009: 3).

A wider perspective is needed – one that recognises that, at every stage of their life, people thrive due to the care they take of themselves and receive from others. In effect, throughout our lives, everyone has a package of care – an ever-changing balance of the five main elements.

Early in life, most people largely care for themselves, supplementing this with companionship and psychological support drawn from family, friends and neighbours, illustrated in Figure 4.5.

A little later in life, as gardening, household maintenance and similar tasks become physically onerous and/or it is difficult to find the time to undertake these, individuals may engage commercial providers or perhaps ask family members to help. Support at this point will normally be self-funded or freely given. The balance of care starts to shift, as illustrated at Figure 4.6. This support is unlikely to be thought of as 'care', even though this meets the dictionary definition which is to *provide physical needs, help or comfort* (Collins 2001: 224).

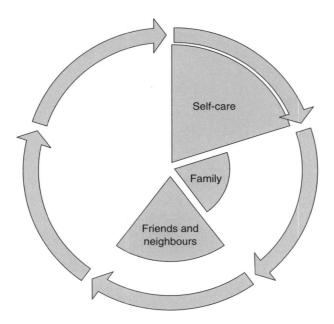

Figure 4.5 Early life

With increasing years, help might be sought for additional tasks such as cleaning and ironing and individuals may start to use community transport, come to rely on ready-made meals and join lunch clubs. This shift continues to enable individuals to stay in their own homes and maintain their quality of life. The balance shifts to that shown in Figure 4.7.

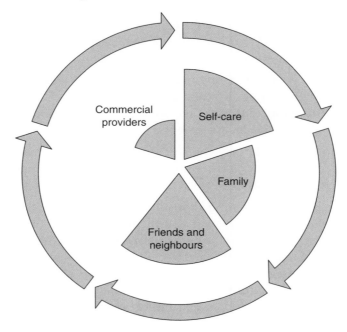

Figure 4.6 Middle years

Figure 4.7 Later years

Later still, personal help might be needed with dressing, feeding and bathing, at which point local authorities are often involved, assessing need and providing advice and equipment. Individuals may make increasing demands on other services, including GPs, paramedics and the local Accident and Emergency department. Remaining in their homes, individuals come to rely on a complex network of informal and formal care but still exercise a degree of self-care (Figure 4.8). At this point, depending on eligibility criteria and personal resources, local authorities may make direct payments and/or secure services for the individual.

Towards the end of their life, a relatively small number of older people develop intense and complex physical, mental and emotional health needs. Residential care is often necessary. If the need for care involves a significant health element, the NHS contributes to or meets the full cost, at which point self-care is likely to be very low. Friend and neighbour support falls away and family support is limited to visiting and perhaps discharging responsibilities such as power of attorney. Figure 4.9 shows the final care package, the cost of which may fall entirely on the state because the level of health need determines the care should be free or the client's funds have been depleted to the point where the individual is no longer able to contribute to the cost of care.

The balance of elements in a person's care package varies over time, as do the financial implications for the state. From a financial perspective, the combination of sociological trends and economic circumstances makes it highly desirable to keep the balance of care skewed towards self- and informal care as long as possible. It is helpful that from a care perspective it is desirable, as individuals retain greater choice, control and independence.

Taking the wider definition of care and support, it is essential that commissioning conversations extend beyond those services that have traditionally been provided

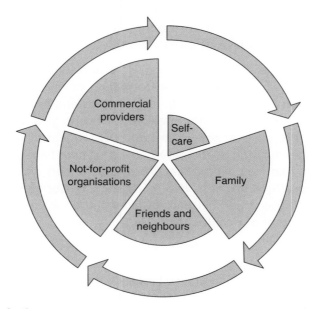

Figure 4.8 The frail years

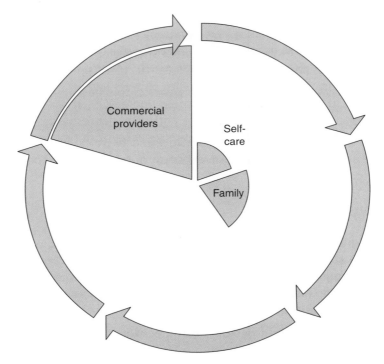

Figure 4.9 The acute years

or procured. Typically, these services offer formal care that is relatively expensive and supports people relatively late in their care journey. Informal care, which starts much earlier in the care journey, is relatively inexpensive to the state and can make a significant contribution to the wellbeing of a person and community. Programmes, activities and services that stimulate or support care by families, friends, peers and neighbours lever resources from the community into the system and increase the total level of care within the community.

The wider definition of care and support is recognised in the *Caring for Our Future* White Paper which promises transformation of care and support to help people *develop and maintain connections to friends and family* (Department of Health 2012a: 21). Furthermore, it is intended to encourage and support communities *to reach out to those at risk of isolation* (Department of Health 2012a: 21). Also promised is stimulation of *the development of time banks, time credits and other approaches that help people share their time, talents and skills with others in the community* (Department of Health 2012a: 21). Social Impact Bonds and funding to support specialised housing for older and disabled people will also be developed (Department of Health 2012a: 21).

When undertaking the Joint Strategic Needs Assessment and developing Joint Health and Wellbeing Strategies, the newly formed Health and Wellbeing Boards should consider both the actual and potential contribution from each of the five sources of care to achieving the vision for the community. Actions to stimulate or maintain each element are shown in Table 4.2.

Table 4.2 Commissioning considerations

Care element	Implications for commissioning
Self-care	Consideration should be given to how individuals can be helped to care for themselves fully or partly. Providing low-level support to a wide range of people, including the relatively young, makes sense from a care and financial perspective. This support includes education intended to change behaviour that will reduce the need for more intensive care later in life and advice on dealing with low-level practical problems in daily living. Support can also include stimulating the supply of managed residential complexes which tend to have good access and client alarm systems.
Family, friends and neighbours	Availability of these care elements is to an extent down to chance. Families may not live close to the individual needing care; the person may never have developed a network of friends or relationships with neighbours. If there is not a culture of looking out for each other, or a fear of implied future commitment, this form of support may not be available. Consideration should be given to targeted public investment to stimulate and improve resilience in care by family, friends, neighbours and peers. Support includes training, advice, help groups and access to respite care.
Not-for-profit organisations	There is often an element of chance as to the support an individual can access within a community. This can be due to patchy availability, low provider visibility and poor user awareness. A lack of expertise and resources often makes it difficult for these organisations to form and expand. Commissioning processes should involve mapping and assessing the resilience of local resources available to the community. Consideration should be given to targeted support to stimulate and strengthen provision, including pump priming, help with finding premises, professional advice, free or subsidised training places and marketing support.
Commercial providers	An assessment should be made of the health of the provider market. Consideration should be given to whether there is an appropriate range and balance of innovative residential and community services for self- and public-funded service users. Questions should be asked regarding whether services of the required quality are priced to allow an appropriate financial return to providers and realise value for (tax payers') money. Furthermore, is there a strong drive for continuous improvement, or is there a need to intervene directly in any area of the market to stimulate new providers, invigorate existing ones and remedy poor performance?

TIPS FOR SUCCESS

In order to commission successfully, local authorities need to maintain or have access to good-quality information regarding:

- *need within their community;*
- *formal provision in terms of quantity, quality and resilience;*
- *availability of support from not-for-profit organisations;*
- *the extent of informal care available to individuals and groups of service users;*
- *what works best locally in terms of meeting need, reducing the need for and length of formal care and stimulating supply.*

The role of local authorities

With an emphasis on personalisation and micro-commissioning, the need for local government involvement might be questioned, particularly where local care markets work well, everyone understands their roles and responsibilities and they are committed to achieving the best outcomes for users and the community. However, the level of risk associated with leaving social care entirely to market forces is unacceptable, particularly given concerns regarding:

- the level and consistency of care available from family, friends, neighbours and community organisations;
- the range, depth and resilience of commercial providers;
- individuals needing care who lack information, skill or resources needed to make sound decisions about their care;
- safeguarding vulnerable adults.

It is recognised that local government involvement in social care needs to continue but the nature of this needs to shift. *Vision for Adult Social Care* states that *councils have a role in stimulating, managing and shaping the market, supporting communities, voluntary organisations, social enterprises and mutuals to flourish and develop innovative and creative ways of addressing care needs* (Department of Health 2010d: 21). Specifically, it is envisaged that local councils should:

- *play a lead role in their communities* (Department of Health 2010d: 24);
- work to *pool and align funding streams at the local level* (Department of Health 2010d: 24);
- *work with private providers, charities, voluntary organisations, mutuals, social enterprises and user-led organisations, and move away from traditional block contracts* (Department of Health 2010d: 24);
- *examine their arrangements for contracting service providers to ensure that the rules are fair, proportionate and enable micro and small social enterprises, user-led organisations and voluntary organisations to compete to deliver personalised services* (Department of Health 2010d: 24).

The 2012 White Paper *Caring for Our Future* states that:

> *instead of purchasing or providing care and support, authorities will increasingly be expected to take a leadership role in a local area: identifying the needs of the local population, supporting communities to keep people active, empowering people to take control through personal budgets and direct payments, providing information and advice, and ensuring a responsive range of care and support options is available.*

> (Department of Health 2012a: 20)

Future legislation is promised in the White Paper, which will *introduce a clear duty on local authorities to incorporate preventative practice and early intervention into care commissioning and planning* (Department of Health 2012a: 21).

Councils, therefore, have six main roles to play:

1. leading the community to develop a vision, set priorities and commit to action;

2. shaping the market within which commissioning occurs;

3. encouraging collaboration across the care system;

4. levering informal care resources from the wider community into the care system;

5. enabling individuals to micro-commission;

6. commissioning for individuals who are unable or unwilling to do this for themselves.

Shifting thinking and behaviour across the system is central to successful commissioning, as evidenced by Essex County Council, in Case Study 4.1.

CASE STUDY **4.1**

Essex County Council

Essex County Council has a declared intention of becoming 'commissioning-led', the achievement of which requires a shift in culture and mindset.

To assist this process the Strategic Planning and Commissioning leadership team, which is responsible for commissioning adult social care, embarked on a process of briefing staff and nudging their behaviour away from procuring services to commissioning for outcomes.

At the root of this briefing is a stated belief that: 'People who are personally resilient and live in inclusive, mutually supportive communities generally have better outcomes and a better quality of life.' This belief leads to a single key principle that: 'Wherever possible and safe, our role is to stimulate and support a response to come from the individual, their friends, families and communities before looking to develop or commission public sector provision.'

The very clear message to staff is that they should consider all options before resorting to publicly funding services. Whilst the financial imperative to do things differently is clear, the recognition that this should lead to better outcomes for people was seen as vital to winning the hearts and minds of staff.

However, it was recognised that simply declaring beliefs and principles was unlikely to lead to changed thinking and behaviour, so the Strategic Planning and Commissioning leadership team prepared a checklist that staff work through

CASE STUDY 4.1 *continued*

when commissioning. This checklist is then used by senior managers to assess business cases, commissioning plans and decisions.

In respect of one or more outcomes:

- *What can or could citizens do for themselves to reduce, delay or avoid need for support?*
- *What can or could citizens do for themselves by way of self-care?*
- *Can we shape existing activities to achieve additional, alternative and multiple outcomes (e.g. shape falls prevention activity to encourage healthier eating, increased exercise, improved mobility and confidence and reduced social isolation)?*
- *Can we influence behavioural change in communities (e.g. so that they become 'dementia-friendly')?*
- *Can we influence others to deliver sought-after outcomes (e.g. other public sector providers)?*
- *Can we stimulate volunteer activity through advice, training and infrastructure support?*
- *Would it be beneficial to devolve commissioning to individuals or communities (e.g. to stimulate innovation, co-production and/or co-financing)?*
- *Is part or all of a planned or actual response to a desired outcome 'non-statutory' and, therefore, avoidable or a candidate for decommissioning?*
- *Is a shift in thinking required by any stakeholder (e.g. staff and volunteers moving from a 'doing for' to 'enable them' mindset)?*

TIPS FOR SUCCESS

In order for commissioning to become embedded and the potential benefits realised, it is important to:

- *recognise that staff need to understand the benefits of commissioning, why it is being introduced and the underpinning beliefs;*
- *stretch thinking to avoid staff becoming stuck with traditional views of service user needs and outcomes, to challenge assumptions and existing authority responses;*
- *act to effect change in the behaviour of citizens, staff, volunteers and organisational leaders;*
- *embed commissioning thinking in business case preparation and evaluation, service reviews, supplier management, decision making and performance management.*

The challenges of commissioning in this sector

Those leading adult social care are faced with a number of challenges, including how to:

- lead a community in developing vision and priorities in a way that supports and enables rather than determines and dictates what will be commissioned;

- respond to predicted increases in demand for social care within finite public funds;

- unleash resources from within the community to maximise the total care available within a community;

- achieve the best possible alignment between the care that is needed and the care that is available;

- manage the market to ensure service quality, user choice, acceptable financial returns and value for money;

- 'run' the new system in a political environment;

- develop effective Health and Wellbeing Boards;

- collaborate with individuals and organisations across the care and support system;

- achieve the right relationship 'tone' with providers and others;

- develop the commercial competence needed to shape an increasingly complex market and manage the supply chain;

- prompt innovation to cause step improvements in outcomes and performance;

- take difficult and potentially unpopular decisions, for example, withdrawing support from individuals whose needs are now considered to be less of a priority, setting realistic quality standards, service decommissioning and acting when a provider is failing;

- manage relatively new and changing risks associated with commissioning, including potential provider failure, market management and client safeguarding.

Chapter 5
Key challenges for health and social care

Comparison between the NHS and social care systems

Over the last ten years, we have seen a steady convergence of the systems for the NHS and social care. Examples include the development of single management teams across councils and Primary Care Trusts (PCTs), joint commissioning and shared commissioning support, jointly funded public health posts, shared strategies through to common regulatory bodies.

It remains to be seen whether the trend towards convergence will continue to full integration or whether it will stop short of this and the two systems will continue to develop along parallel lines.

As outlined in Table 5.1, the two systems are quite similar, yet differ in certain key respects.

The similarity between health and social care organisations is likely to increase as a result of the Health and Social Care Act 2012, due to greater local political involvement in health arising from the transfer of public health to local government and the establishment of Health and Wellbeing Boards. Rather than removing the national versus local political direction 'divide', it is likely to make it more complex. Inevitably, there will be tensions between the centralist perspective of NHS England and Clinical Commissioning Groups (CCGs) which want to act locally to meet the needs of their local population.

Table 5.1 NHS and social care – similarities and differences

Similarities between NHS and social care	Differences between NHS and social care
• Monitored by many regulatory bodies	• Histories
• Common commitment and statutory duty to work in partnership	• Cultures of 'doing to' in health and 'doing with' in social care
• High and increasing public expectation regarding what is available and cost	• Driven by different political systems; more national in health and more local in social care
• Imbalance between demand and available resources	• Free at the point of delivery versus means-tested
• Problem of getting balance right between frontline, management and support staff	• There is an NHS Constitution but no equivalent for social care
• Increasing use of technology	• Medical staff are more powerful politically than social workers
• Continual pressure to improve performance	• Organisational stability – NHS has undergone repeated large-scale top-down reorganisations whilst local authorities tend to reorganise individually, often in response to ever-reducing budgets
• High political profile	
• Both sectors have become more commercialised and make greater use of private sector providers	
• Difficult issues related to either system are often 'kicked into touch' politically	• Different terms are used to describe those within the community intended to benefit from their services. Whilst *patient* is commonly used within health, in social care a wider variety of terms are found, including *service user, client* and *people*
• Both are developing more personalised, user-centred approaches to commissioning	

Both the trend towards community-based commissioning and the need to focus the agenda more on wellbeing require a 'doing with' approach and it is likely this 'culture' will be adopted across the sectors.

It appears that central government continues to have little real appetite to tackle such 'wicked issues' as free versus means-tested services and the level of personal responsibility required of individuals. For the foreseeable future, the problems caused by not facing up to them will be a central challenge for leaders of both the health and care sectors.

The creation of a National Skills Academy for Social Care, soon to be merged with Skills for Care, the proposed appointment of a Chief Social Worker and other developments are likely to increase the sense of a collective social care profession, increase consistency of practice and standards and increase the voice of social care leaders. At the same time, a multi-professional approach to the education of health professionals is being adopted within the NHS by the formation of Health Education England and local Education and Training Boards comprising provider organisations, often including social care. However, in the short term at least, medical professionals are likely to be more powerful politically.

Whilst future reorganisation of the NHS cannot be ruled out, there appears to be little appetite for any national reconfiguration of local government. However, a combination of localism, community budgeting and reduced funding is likely to result in a diversity of local arrangements and many smaller-scale reorganisations.

The specific challenges facing the NHS and social care

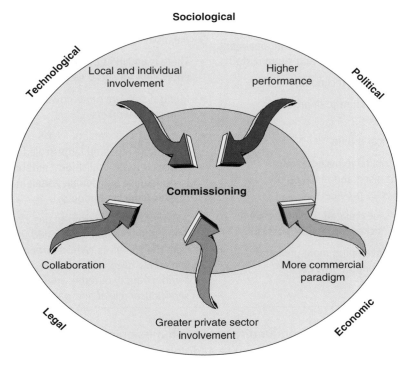

Figure 5.1 Commissioning environment

Financial

Despite additional investment in the NHS, and attempts to improve efficiency through programmes such as Quality, Innovation, Productivity and Prevention (QIPP), current demand continues to outstrip supply. This is before we factor in the continuing growth in population and the increasingly complex needs of people living longer.

Medical advances mean the range of possible interventions for patients are so much greater than they were in 1948. Increasingly, members of the public expect to receive any and every possible treatment for free. The NHS cannot afford to do all that they would like to do. An adult debate is urgently needed nationally to define the core level of service which the twenty-first-century NHS is able to provide realistically and what services people should expect to pay for on a means-tested basis, personally or via some form of medical insurance. Clinicians, particularly doctors, are probably in the strongest position to lead this public debate, as traditionally they are considered the profession which is most trusted by the public (Ipsos MORI/BMA, 2011). A similar national debate is needed in respect of social care, which faces two similar challenges – how to address:

• the significant projected increases in the number of clients presenting with needs which cannot be resourced by local authorities in traditional ways; and

• the level of financial contribution that should be expected from clients and, potentially, their families.

The current system is complicated, confusing and inequitable and needs to be tackled.

For the future survival of both institutions, much greater emphasis needs to be given to prevention and wellbeing rather than cure and care. This is central to the role of the new Health and Wellbeing Boards which are now being established by every county or unitary council in England. The various campaigns for topics such as healthier eating, wellbeing at work, smoking cessation, breastfeeding and the importance of regular exercise are set to be the norm. A new understanding is needed of responsibilities and rights with a clear emphasis on self-care, informal care by family, friends and neighbours, community-organised services and charity support. Public sector organisations should take more of a strategic role, managing the formal care provider market, stimulating and supporting self-care and informal care, and directly commissioning services to address outcomes that cannot be achieved in any other way.

The quality of leadership

Effective commissioning requires leadership of a very high quality. Everyone involved needs:

• skills associated with the 16 activities detailed in Chapter 2, as relevant to their role;

• an ability to collaborate across the system;

• to understand how other stakeholders operate from professional, managerial and political perspectives;

• a degree of commercial acumen.

Clinicians, in particular GPs, have the opportunity to lead the way in which healthcare is delivered in their communities both as commissioners but also as co-leaders, with their clinical colleagues in self-governing Foundation Trusts. It is particularly important that the quality of clinical leadership across primary and secondary care improves in order to enable seamless patient pathways to be possible. To do this, leadership has to become a compulsory element of medical education, much greater than, for example, the current 'tick in the box' approach as registrars near the end of their training.

Ten years ago, some hospital consultants would firmly deny that management had anything to do with being a clinician. Most had little, if any, idea of how leadership worked in their own organisations, let alone what they might be able to do to influence it. Similarly, in the early stages of GP commissioning, some GPs clearly believed that all they needed to do was turn up at the board meeting from time to time, say very little and then leave. They failed to understand the key role which boards play, the importance of having constructive debate, making effective decisions and then representing the 'corporate' view when they are operating outside.

There are already signs that this is changing. It is noticeable amongst doctors in training now that leadership is viewed much more seriously and an increasing number of specialist registrars are studying for MBAs alongside their clinical training. At a local level, GP leaders of some of the new CCGs have quickly realised the importance of working closely with clinical colleagues in local hospitals, mental health and community service providers to plan the future and overcome the problems and prejudices of the past. In East Suffolk, for example, the local CCG has started developing joint arrangements for service planning and redesign as well as joint leadership training across primary and secondary care.

GPs, in general, and practice managers, in particular, are likely to possess a degree of commercial experience and acumen so this aspect of their personal development is perhaps less of a challenge than understanding how other stakeholders operate, how to plan in a bigger strategic and political context and how to collaborate across the system.

Many social care leaders are accustomed to working with private providers and have collaborated with health colleagues for some time. These leaders have a degree of understanding of commercial operation and health organisations and are used to working in a political environment. However, future commissioning will involve a more strategic involvement in the community and market and require much greater collaboration. Commercial acumen will also be required.

Technology

For both sectors, we are likely to see technology play a much greater part in future. It is already having an enormous impact on the provision of services themselves, such as the development of 'smart homes' where people can be monitored remotely and the application of stem cell research to curing disease and rehabilitation. It also has a major part to play in the way in which people access the services through provision of better public education, greater use of Skype, telephone, text and email for communicating with patients and service users and the collection of relevant data to support decision making and engagement.

Outcomes focus

The most recent changes put much greater emphasis on the outcomes of health and social care rather than outputs and inputs. The NHS and social care organisations will be judged much more on results, which should reduce considerably the current bureaucratic burden of multiple monitoring and help everyone remember that commissioning and providing are not ends in themselves but, rather, a means to improving people's health and wellbeing.

In the past, health commissioning has tended to be organised around the contractual arrangements, i.e. by provider, rather than the patient (Civitas 2010) and typically proportional spend looks like Figure 5.2.

If we are to move to a more outcomes-focused culture, we will need to take a range of different perspectives such as the proportion of money spent by:

1. Age groups (Figure 5.3);

2. Geography/local needs (Figure 5.4);

3. Location of services, i.e. where they are delivered (Figure 5.5);

4. Prevention and wellbeing versus cure and care (Figure 5.6);

5. People's life pathways (Figure 5.7).

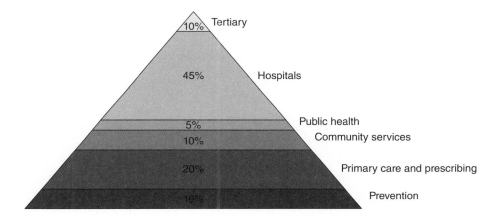

Figure 5.2 Proportional spend by type of provider

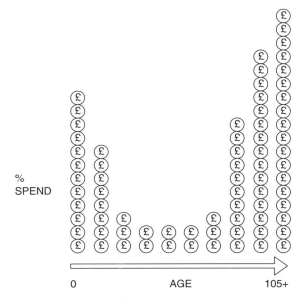

Figure 5.3 Proportional spend by age group of patient/user

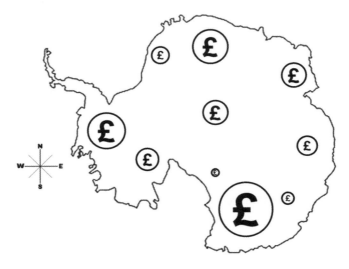

Figure 5.4 Proportional spend by geography/local needs

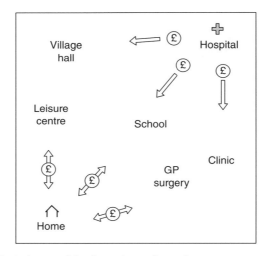

Figure 5.5 Proportional spend by location of services

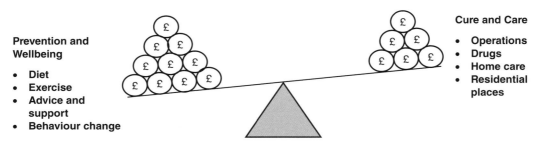

Figure 5.6 Proportional spend between prevention and wellbeing versus cure and care

Figure 5.7 Proportional spend by people's life pathways (NHSCB)

Challenging old behaviour

Many of those involved in health and social care will find commissioning requires a shift in thinking. The ease with which this shift is made will vary from person to person as it affects a number of aspects of how they view the world, including potentially:

- Needing to work with private sector providers which some may assume have different priorities and values. There is a risk of providers being portrayed as only concerned with money, which is unhelpful and, for the most part, untrue. Leaving aside their personal values and motivations for being in the care profession, if providers are to survive beyond the very short term, they have to focus on delivering quality care. As commissioners become more skilled, individual citizens enabled and competition increases, providers will need to demonstrate that they deliver value for money. Some providers will choose to offer very high-quality treatment and care at a commensurately high price whilst others will offer lower, but acceptable, levels of quality at a cheaper price.

- Having less direct involvement with patients and clients and more with providers. In the longer term, it is likely that the number of staff employed by commissioning organisations will fall and those that remain will have little direct contact with patients or clients. Those staff with commissioning roles, who particularly value this direct contact, will need to come to terms with this new reality. Some are likely to seek employment with a provider organisation.

- Thinking in terms of markets, financial return and competition. This can feel rather cold and detached from the patient and client experience, especially when this is what motivated the individual to enter the health and social care professions in the first place.

- Enabling clients to make their own choices. This involves some suppression of what is for some people a natural wish to use professional knowledge to help a client.

As we have shown, NHS England officially recognises the importance of CCGs needing to behave differently from the previous PCTs and for them to have time to mature. It is important that this attitude and approach are backed up by NHS England's own behaviour, as it will largely set the tone for the NHS. Each CCG is required to have an Organisational Development Plan to demonstrate how it will develop the skills and knowledge required to lead the wider health economy effectively. What is not clear is whether NHS England is required to have one too.

Equally, behaviour needs to change at a local level. The dominant 'top-down' nature of NHS leadership has tended to produce a largely passive culture where organisations tend to wait for guidance and then react to it rather than to think things through for themselves and then take responsibility for their own actions. The NHS has a strong reputation for initiatives such as Clinical Governance (Scally and Donaldson 1998: 61–65), World Class Commissioning (Department of Health 2009), Foundation Trusts (Health and Social Care (Community Health and Standards) Act 2003), CCG authorisation (NHS Commissioning Board 2012) or QIPP (Department of Health 2011). Too often, these quickly becoming synonymous with lots of long, unproductive meetings, unwieldy committees and task forces, someone's lead responsibility. Instead it needs to mean effective management of scarce resources in which everyone has a part to play. A system led by local leaders will require them to take responsibility for their own actions and the consequences. We cannot afford a national bureaucratic 'monitoring machine'.

Once again, the extent to which clinicians invest time in their own leadership training will be a critical factor. It is interesting to note the growing interest of doctors in training in leadership development. Many now see this as an essential part of their wider development as clinicians. They are recognising early on the importance of having influence within the system and, to have this, they need both the skills and to understand the system. Some organisations, such as the South Essex Partnership NHS Foundation Trust, are responding by promoting clinicians into leadership roles much earlier in their careers than has been the case previously.

In particular, we need to see a change in the often adversarial behavior between local commissioners and providers which is often fuelled by defensive contracts. For health and social care economies to be more stable and for better-quality services to be available, we need relational contracts which recognise the importance of regular dialogue between the parties and early mediation when needed rather than rushing to resolve expensive legal disputes. Leadership development for clinicians across both commissioning and provider organisations, whatever sector they operate in, would help to build greater mutual understanding and trust.

Local and individual involvement

The imbalance between demand and supply also increases the need for the public to take more responsibility for their own health and wellbeing as well as being able to exert their rights. There is already evidence of GPs making treatment, such as major surgery, conditional upon people losing weight or stopping smoking because of the evidence of poor prognosis in such cases. These policies are currently managed at a local level; they would be more powerful if a collaborative approach could be adopted by CCGs working together at a regional or, preferably, national level, especially where they are developed in conjunction with the public.

The opportunities for the public to get involved with the development of health and social care have been very fragmented. Often, this hassled people into either accepting their lot or resorting quickly to direct contact with politicians or the media. Politicians are very conscious of the importance of reducing any risks to patient safety due to poor local services and this is reflected in the changes to the local Healthwatch organisations which can monitor both health and social care services, the increasing powers being given to members and governors of Foundation Trusts, the need for all general practices to have patient participation groups and regular surveys and the lay representation on the new CCG governing bodies. The development of a national network of local Healthwatch organisations is an opportunity to change this if it can be managed well. Their influence has been strengthened in particular by the link Healthwatch England will have to the Care Quality Commission at a national level.

GP leaders of CCGs, in particular, have to learn the importance of broadening their perspective from individual patients or groups of patients to the community and wider population needs.

We also need to see greater employee involvement in the commissioning and provision of services. Too often, staff providing services operate in a 'service vacuum' with little or no understanding of where their clients or patients come from or go to after they have seen them. Greater involvement of different professionals in pathway design could go a long way to improving the overall care experience and reducing incidents of poor-quality hand-offs within the health and social care system.

Collaboration

To achieve integrated, seamless services, we need different professionals who are employed by different organisations to collaborate for the benefit of their local population. Collaboration, as stated earlier, is vital to the future of the NHS and social care. Collaboration between the public and commissioners, the public and providers, between different commissioners (including local councils), between commissioners and providers and between providers is fairly well accepted. Collaboration now needs to extend to include family, friends and neighbours providing informal care as well as clients and patients.

The reality is that the NHS and social care are still largely two separate systems with different histories, cultures, languages and customs. A significant challenge therefore comes from commissioners and providers tending to work in silos, each having knowledge of their own service but little knowledge about anyone else's or the interdependence of the different organisations. A fundamental part of any clinician's professional training should be to understand NHS and local government's politics, structures, financing and decision-making processes and their alignment.

Working with local councils is very new for most GPs who previously may have had little or nothing to do with them. The challenge remains how to integrate health and social care needs effectively through better joint commissioning and joint provision and ensuring the local public understand how to use what is available effectively. The council-led Health and Wellbeing Board is now the principal gateway for GPs to understand the broader world of public service. It can help them to engage more widely with partners such as further and higher education, police, fire and rescue services, trading standards, Job Centre Plus and the criminal justice system, including the probation and prison services.

Effective commissioning and contract management

Social care leaders have many years of experience letting and managing contracts with voluntary and private sector providers, usually supported by procurement professionals. Commissioning however is a much more significant process than simply letting and managing contacts. Community visioning, identifying and prioritising need, resource mapping, innovation and service design all need to occur before contracts can be let. In addition, commissioners need to manage population need, markets and providers.

In order for health and social care organisations to commission successfully, agency leaders need to address three key ingredients: frameworks, processes and competent staff (Figure 5.8).

Frameworks are the rules and regulations within which commissioning will occur and include the NHS Constitution, eligibility criteria, arrangements for local governance and financial regulations. Processes are needed for data gathering, analysis and synthesis, managing the market, letting and managing contracts, evaluation and learning. Sufficient staff who possess the skills needed for effective commissioning and collaboration are similarly vital to success. Depending on the approach to commissioning and the degree to which this is intended to be culturally embedded, different people need different skills. It is essential in future

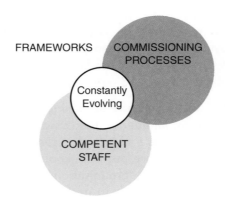

Figure 5.8 Successful commissioning: three key ingredients

that all clinicians and social care professionals understand what commissioning means in practice, whether they work for a commissioning, provider or combined commissioner/provider organisation. Traditionally, many clinicians have tended to argue that the split of responsibilities has meant that this was of no relevance to them. This attitude tends to change when clinicians realise that their salaries depend on effective commissioning.

Where commissioning is embedded in the culture, three main groups of staff are evident.

1. a relatively small group of senior staff responsible for environmental scanning, reviewing internal and external learning and sensing how commissioning frameworks, processes and skills need to evolve. This group will challenge current performance and act to improve the wider culture so that commissioning becomes and remains effective;

2. professionals such as accountants, lawyers and procurement experts, able to deploy their expertise in a commissioning context;

3. health and social care professionals and managers who understand need, outcomes, service design and quality and professional practice.

A number of CCGs are already actively engaging their GP member practices in service development but there will also be the need to recognise that, once new service designs are agreed and commissioned, the practices need to ensure they happen. Equally, if services do not work well, GPs have a responsibility to feed back concerns and take an active part in putting things right.

Too often in the past, in the NHS, large provider organisations have been able to play off one commissioner against another. Collaboration and trust between commissioners will be essential to future success. When it comes to deciding the geography of any CCG, size will matter in terms of their influence, market leverage and economies of scale.

The CCGs have a particular challenge of working out which activities should be carried out by the CCG itself and how it will function internally within a budget of £25 per head of population. This sum is considerably lower than the previous PCT budget and calls for ingenuity and a strong cooperative culture. As well as needing to be good at commissioning health services, the CCG needs to be good at commissioning its own support in order to carry out that commissioning.

What questions do we need to answer?

The move to commissioning raises many questions, some of which relate to the overall system and need to be answered by national or senior local leaders and others by those involved more personally and operationally.

However skilled in commissioning individuals are, if wider questions about the system are not addressed the full benefits will not be realised.

The questions in Table 5.2 are intended to prompt thought, discussion and action by those in a position to help establish the new arrangements and for those required to operate within them.

The questions in Table 5.3 are aimed at those operationally involved in commissioning.

Table 5.2 Wider system questions

1	What are we prepared to do to manage the growing imbalance between the demand for treatment and care and available resources?
2	What core level of service and what standard of service quality can we afford to provide in both the NHS and social care?
3	Which services should be free at the point of delivery? Which should be means-tested and how much should be charged?
4	What do we need to do to align the core values underpinning the NHS and social care and move to a 'doing with', personalised common culture?
5	What do we need to do to ensure there is a balance between improving health and wellbeing on the Health and Wellbeing Boards?
6	What do we need to do to achieve truly effective multi-agency collaboration, particularly between the NHS and social care, in terms of both commissioning and provision?
7	What do we need to do to facilitate effective wider collaboration so that individuals are properly engaged in their own care?
8	What do we need to do to move to more outcomes-focused commissioning?
9	What do we need to do to ensure good governance with minimum bureaucracy?
10	What competences are needed for effective commissioning in our local system?

Table 5.3 Personal questions

1	What is my role with regard to commissioning and how might this develop?
2	How does my contribution fit within the wider health and social care economy?
3	What can I do differently in future to help the system to be more effective?
4	What do I need to stop doing?
5	How might I lead in the new system?
6	How can I influence the system appropriately?
7	Which relationships are critical to me being effective?
8	What behaviours and skills do I require?
9	How do I develop these behaviours and skills?
10	How do I balance public sector values with working in a commercial environment?

Conclusion

None of these factors are new – they have run like golden threads through the NHS and social care systems for at least the last 15 years. What is different this time is the threat of the economic circumstances we find ourselves in. Local government now has to deal with drastic budget reductions, and while the NHS funding has politically been ring-fenced, it still has to find year-on-year savings of between 6 to 8 per cent per annum if it is to be able to maintain its current level of service, taking account of national terms and conditions, ever-increasing utility bills and higher than average medical inflation rates. If we consider the effects of a population growing in size and complexity, the challenge is financially even greater.

If we do not face these challenges now and together, the NHS and social care systems as we currently know them will spiral into disrepute and fail. Some would say it is already happening.

As we head closer to the next general election in 2015, the opposition is already suggesting an even stronger role for local government in healthcare. It remains to be seen how courageous our politicians will be in facing the twin problems of increasing social care and NHS costs and leading a step-change in the way we manage these issues. Year-on-year budget reductions do not lend themselves to innovation; yet, innovation is what is needed now before the system implodes completely.

As we said at the beginning of our text, we need the best of both worlds across the political spectrum as well as across health and social care.

Appendix 1
Glossary of terms

ACEVO	Association of Chief Executives of Voluntary Organisations
BMA	British Medical Association
CBI	Confederation of British Industry
CCG	Clinical Commissioning Group
CCT	compulsory competitive tendering
CQC	Care Quality Commission
DLO	direct labour organisation
DSO	direct service organisation
GP	general practitioner
JSNA	Joint Strategic Needs Assessment
LGA	Local Government Association
LINks	Local Involvement Networks
NHS	National Health Service
NHSCBA/NHSCB	NHS Commissioning Board
PCG	Primary Care Group
PCT	Primary Care Trust
PEC	Professional Executive Committee
QIPP	Quality, Innovation, Productivity and Prevention
SHA	Strategic Health Authority

Appendix 2
NHS Constitution

The NHS Constitution belongs to the people and establishes the principles and values of the NHS in England. It sets out rights to which patients, public and staff are entitled, and pledges which the NHS is committed to achieve, together with responsibilities which the public, patients and staff owe to one another to ensure that the NHS operates fairly and effectively. All NHS bodies and private and third sector providers supplying NHS services are required by law to take account of this Constitution in their decisions and actions. The Constitution will be renewed every 10 years, with the involvement of the public, patients and staff.

The Handbook to the NHS Constitution which accompanies it will be renewed at least every three years, setting out current guidance on the rights, pledges, duties and responsibilities established by the Constitution. These requirements for renewal are legally binding.

1 Principles that guide the NHS
1.1 The NHS provides a comprehensive service available to all

- Duty to each and every individual that it serves and must respect their human rights;

- Wider social duty to promote equality through the services it provides and to pay particular attention to groups or sections of society where improvements in health and life expectancy are not keeping pace with the rest of the population.

1.2 Access to NHS services based on clinical need, not an individual's ability to pay

- NHS services are free of charge, except in limited circumstances sanctioned by Parliament.

1.3 The NHS aspires to the highest standards of excellence and professionalism

- Provision of high-quality care that is safe, effective and focused on patient experience;

- Planning and delivery of clinical and other services it provides;
- The people it employs and the education, training and development they receive;
- Commitment to innovation and the promotion and conduct of research to improve the current and future health and care of the population.

1.4 NHS services must reflect the needs and preferences of patients, their families and their carers

- Will be involved in and consulted with, where appropriate on all decisions about their care and treatment.

1.5 NHS works across organisational boundaries and in partnership with other organisations in the interest of patients, local communities and the wider population

1.6 NHS is committed to providing best value for taxpayers' money and the most effective, fair and sustainable use of finite resources

1.7 NHS is accountable to the public, communities and patients that it serves

- System of responsibility and accountability for taking decisions in the NHS should be transparent and clear to the public, patients and staff.

2a Patients and the public – your rights and NHS pledges to you

Everyone who uses the NHS should understand what legal rights they have and what to do if they think that they have not received what is rightfully theirs.

The Constitution also contains pledges that the NHS is committed to achieve. Pledges go beyond legal rights. This means that pledges are not legally binding but represent a commitment by the NHS to provide high-quality services.

Access to health services

You have the right:

- to receive NHS services free of charge, apart from central limited exceptions sanctioned by Parliament;
- to access NHS services. You will not be refused access on unreasonable grounds;
- to expect your local NHS to access the requirements of the local community and to commission and put in place the services to meet those needs as considered necessary;

- in certain circumstances, to go to other European Economic Area countries or Switzerland for treatment, which would be available to you through your NHS commissioner;

- not to be unlawfully discriminated against in the provision of NHS services including on grounds of gender, race, religion or belief, sexual orientation, disability (including learning disability or mental illness) or age;

- to access services within maximum waiting times, or for the NHS to take all reasonable steps to offer you a range of alternative providers if this is not possible. The waiting times are described in the Handbook to the NHS Constitution;

- to provide convenient, easy access to services within the waiting times set out in the Handbook to the NHS Constitution (pledge);

- to make decisions in a clear and transparent way, so that patients and the public can understand how services are planned and delivered (pledge); and

- to make the transition as smooth as possible when you are referred between services, and to include you in relevant discussions (pledge).

Quality of care and environment

You have the right:

- to accept or refuse treatment that is offered to you, and not to be given any physical examination or treatment unless you have given valid consent. If you do not have the capacity to do so, consent must be obtained from a person legally able to act on your behalf, or the treatment must be in your best interests;

- to be given information about your proposed treatment in advance, including any significant risks and any alternative treatments which may be available, and the risks involved in doing nothing;

- to privacy and confidentiality and to expect the NHS to keep your confidential information safe and secure;

- of access to your own health records. These will always be used to manage your treatment in your best interests.

The NHS also commits:

- to share with you any letters sent between clinicians about your care (pledge).

Informed choice

You have the right:

- to choose your GP practice, and to be accepted by that practice unless there are reasonable grounds to refuse, in which case you will be informed of those reasons;

- to express a preference for using a particular doctor within your GP practice, and for the practice to try and comply;
- to make choices about your NHS care and to information to support these choices. The options available to you will develop over time and depend on your individual needs. Details are set out in the Handbook to the NHS Constitution.

The NHS also commits:

- to inform you about the healthcare services available to you, locally and nationally (pledge); and
- to offer you easily accessible, reliable and relevant information to enable you to participate fully in your own healthcare decisions and to support you in making choices. This will include information on the quality of clinical services where there is robust and accurate information available (pledge).

Involvement in your healthcare and in the NHS

You have the right:

- to be involved in discussions and decisions about your healthcare, and to be given information to enable you to do this;
- to be involved, directly or through representatives, in the planning of health-care services, the development and consideration of proposals for changes in the way those services are provided, and in decisions to be made affecting the operation of those services.

The NHS also commits:

- to provide you with the information you need to influence and scrutinise the planning and delivery of NHS services (pledge); and
- to work in partnership with you, your family, carers and representatives (pledge).

Complaint and redress

You have the right:

- to have any complaint you make about NHS services dealt with efficiently and to have it properly investigated;
- to know the outcome of any investigation into your complaint;
- to take your complaint to the independent Health Service Ombudsman, if you are not satisfied with the way your complaint has been dealt with by the NHS;
- to make a claim for judicial review if you think you have been directly affected by an unlawful act or decision of an NHS body;
- to compensation where you have been harmed by negligent treatment.

The NHS also commits to:

- ensure you are treated with courtesy and you receive appropriate support throughout the handling of a complaint; and the fact that you have complained will not adversely affect your future treatment (pledge);

- acknowledge mistakes when they happen, apologise, explain what went wrong and put things right quickly and effectively (pledge);

- ensure that the organisation learns lessons from complaints and claims and uses these to improve NHS services (pledge).

2b Patients and the public – your responsibilities

The NHS belongs to all of us. There are things that we can all do for ourselves and for one another to help it work effectively, and to ensure resources are used responsibly.

You should recognise that you can make a significant contribution to your own health and your family's good health and wellbeing, and take some personal responsibility for it.

You should:

- **register with a GP practice;**

- **treat NHS staff and other patients with respect;**

- **provide accurate information** about your health, condition and status;

- **keep appointments,** or cancel within reasonable time;

- **follow the course of treatment** which you have agreed;

- **participate** in important public health programmes such as vaccination;

- **ensure** that those closest to you are aware of your wishes about organ donation;

- **give feedback** – both positive and negative – about the treatment and care you have received.

3a Staff – your rights and NHS pledges to you

It is the commitment, professionalism and dedication of staff working for the benefit of the people the NHS serves which really make the difference. High-quality care requires high-quality workplaces, with commissioners and providers aiming to be employers of choice.

- All staff (clinicians and non-clinicians) should have rewarding and worthwhile jobs, with the freedom and confidence to act in the best interests of patients. To do this, they must be treated with respect at work, have the tools, training and support to deliver care and opportunities to develop and progress.

Staff have extensive legal rights embodied in general employment and discrimi-nation law. In addition, individual contracts of employment contain terms and conditions giving staff further rights.

The rights are there to help ensure that staff:

- have a good working environment with flexible working opportunities, con-sistent with the needs of patients and with the way that people live their lives;
- have fair pay and contract framework;
- can be involved and represented in the workplace;
- have healthy and safe working conditions and an environment free from har-assment, bullying or violence;
- are treated fairly, equally and free from discrimination; and
- can raise an internal grievance and if necessary seek redress, where it is felt that a right has not been upheld.

In addition to these legal rights, the NHS are committed to achieving a number of **pledges**.

The NHS commits to:

- provide all staff with clear roles and responsibilities and rewarding jobs for teams and individuals that make a difference to patients, their families and carers and communities;
- provide all staff with personal development, access to appropriate training for their jobs and line management support to succeed;
- provide support and opportunities for staff to maintain their health, wellbeing and safety;
- engage staff in decisions that affect them and the services they provide, indi-vidually, through representative organisations and through local partnership working arrangements. All staff will be empowered to put forward ways to deliver better and safer services for patients and their families.

3b Staff – your responsibilities

All staff have responsibilities to the public, their patients and colleagues.

Important legal duties summarised

You have a duty:

- to accept professional accountability and maintain the standards of profes-sional practice as set by the appropriate regulatory body applicable to your profession or role;
- to take reasonable care of health and safety at work for you, your team and others, and to cooperate with employers to ensure compliance with health and safety requirements;

- to act in accordance with the express and implied terms of your contract of employment;

- not to discriminate against patients or staff and to adhere to equal opportunities and equality and human rights legislation;

- to protect the confidentiality of personal information that you hold unless to do so would put anyone at risk of significant harm;

- to be honest and truthful in applying for a job and in carrying out that job.

The Constitution also includes expectations that reflect how staff should play their part in ensuring the success of the NHS and delivering high-quality care.

You should aim to:

- maintain the highest standards of care and service, taking responsibility not only for the care you personally provide, but also for your wider contribution to the aims of your team and the NHS as a whole;

- take up training and development opportunities provided over and above those legally required of your post;

- play your part in sustainability, improving services by working in partnership with patients, the public and communities;

- be open with patients, their families, carers or representatives, including if anything goes wrong; welcoming and listening to feedback and addressing concerns promptly and in a spirit of cooperation. You should contribute to a climate where the truth can be heard and the reporting of, and learning from, errors is encouraged; and

- view the services you provide from the standpoint of a patient, and involve patients, their families and carers in the services you provide, working with them, their communities and other organisations, and making it clear who is responsible for their care.

NHS values

Patients, public and staff have helped develop this expression of values that inspire passion in the NHS and should guide it in the twenty-first century. Individual organisations will develop and refresh their own values, tailored to their local needs. The NHS values provide common ground for cooperation to achieve shared aspirations:

- respect and dignity;

- commitment to quality of care;

- compassion;

- improving lives;

- working together for patients;

- everyone counts.

Appendix 3
Nolan principles of public life

Selflessness

Holders of public office should act solely in terms of the public interest.

Integrity

Holders of public office should not place themselves under any financial or other obligation to outside individuals or organisations that might seek to influence them in the performance of their official duties.

Objectivity

In carrying out public business, including making public appointments, awarding contracts or recommending individuals for rewards and benefits, holders of public office should make choices on merit.

Accountability

Holders of public office are accountable for their decisions and actions to the public and must submit themselves to whatever scrutiny is appropriate to their office.

Openness

Holders of public office should be as open as possible about decisions and actions that they take. They should give reasons for their decisions and restrict information only when the wider public interest clearly demands.

Honesty

Holders of public office have a duty to declare any private interests relating to their public duties and to take steps to resolve any conflicts arising in a way that protects the public interest.

Leadership

Holders of public office should promote and support these principles by leadership and example.

References

ACEVO (2012) *The Complete Dictionary of Commissioning and Procurement* [online] www.acevo.org.uk/commissioning.

Association of Directors of Social Services (2003) *All Our Tomorrows, Inverting the Triangle of Care* [online] www.adass.org.uk.

Association of Directors of Social Services (2012a) *A New System for Care Funding. 'Now Is the Time to Act'* [online] www.adass.org.uk.

Association of Directors of Social Services (2012b) *Use of Personal Budgets Leaps by Nearly 40%* [online] www.adass.org.uk.

Audit Commission (1996) *What the Doctor Ordered – A Study of GP Fundholders in England and Wales.* London: HMSO.

Audit Commission (1998) *A Fruitful Partnership – Effective Partnership Working.* London: Audit Commission.

British Political Speeches (2010) [online] www.britishpoliticalspeech.org/speech-archive.htm?speech=32.

Care Services Improvement Partnership (2006) *Commissioning Book – Chapter 1: The Commissioning Context* [online] https://www.gov.uk/government/publications/commissioning-e-book-care-services-improvement-partnership-2006.

Care Services Improvement Partnership (2007) *Children's Commissioning Development Workshop Briefing Papers* [online] www.chimat.org.uk/resource/view.aspx?RID=57828.

CBI/LGA (2009) *Commissioning Strategically for Better Public Services Across Local Government* [online] www.cbi.org.uk.

Central Procurement Directorate (2012) *Procurement Guidance Note 07/04 – Strategic Procurement* [online] www.dfpni.gov.uk/index/procurement.

Civitas (2010) *Refusing Treatment.*

Clark, G (2010) *Growing the Big Society* [online] https://www.gov.uk/government/speeches/growing-the-big-society--2.

Collins (2001) *Concise English Dictionary – 21st Century Edition,* 5th edn. Glasgow: Harper Collins.

Commissioning Support Programme (2009) *Achieving Better Outcomes – Commissioning in Children's Services* [online] http://dorsetyouth.com/commissioning_in_children39s_services_csp1.pdf.

Commissioning Support Programme (2010) *Good Commissioning Principles and Practice* [online] www.commissioningsupport.org.uk.

Competition and Co-operation Panel (2010) *Fast Track Report: Merger of NHS Oxfordshire's Provider Arm and Oxfordshire and Buckinghamshire Mental Health NHS Foundation Trust,* November.

Department for Communities and Local Government (2009) *Empowering Communities, Shaping Prospects, Transforming Lives – A Vision for Intelligent Commissioning in Local Government* (Informal Consultation Draft).

Department for Communities and Local Government (2012) *Statistical Release – Local Authority Expenditure and Financing England 2012–13 Budget*. London: Department for Communities and Local Government.

Department of Health (1997) *The New NHS: Modern, Dependable*. White Paper [online] http://webarchive.nationalarchives.gov.uk.

Department of Health (1999) *Primary Care Trusts: Establishment, the Preparatory Period and Their Functions* [online] http://webarchive.nationalarchives.gov.uk.

Department of Health (2000) *NHS Plan – A Plan for Investment, A Plan for Reform* [online] http://webarchive.nationalarchives.gov.uk.

Department of Health (2001) *Shifting the Balance of Power Within the NHS: Securing Delivery* [online] http://webarchive.nationalarchives.gov.uk.

Department of Health (2003) *Fair Access to Care Services – Guidance on Eligibility Criteria for Adult Social Care* [online] http://webarchive.nationalarchives.gov.uk.

Department of Health (2004) *NHS Improvement Plan* [online] http://webarchive.nationalarchives.gov.uk.

Department of Health (2005a) *Creating a Patient-Led NHS Delivering the NHS Improvement Plan* [online] http://webarchive.nationalarchives.gov.uk.

Department of Health (2005b) *Commissioning a Patient-Led NHS* [online] http://webarchive.nationalarchives.gov.uk.

Department of Health (2006) *Transforming Community Services: Enabling New Patterns of Provision* [online] http://webarchive.nationalarchives.gov.uk.

Department of Health (2007a) *Primary Care Trusts Professional Executive Committees – Fit for Future* [online] http://webarchive.nationalarchives.gov.uk.

Department of Health (2007b) *Our NHS, Our Future: NHS Next Stage Review Interim Report* [online] http://webarchive.nationalarchives.gov.uk.

Department of Health (2007c) *World Class Commissioning (a) – Competencies* [online] www.dh.gov.uk.

Department of Health (2007d) *World Class Commissioning: Vision* [online] http://webarchive.nationalarchives.gov.uk.

Department of Health (2008) *High Quality Care for All: NHS Next Stage Review Final Report* [online] http://webarchive.nationalarchives.gov.uk.

Department of Health (2009) *World Class Commissioning: An Introduction* [online] http://webarchive.nationalarchives.gov.uk.

Department of Health (2010a) *Equity and Excellence: Liberating the NHS*, July 2010 *and Liberating the NHS – Legislative Framework and Next Steps*, December 2010.

Department of Health (2010b) *Robert Francis Inquiry Report into Mid-Staffordshire NHS Foundation Trust*. London: The Stationery Office.

Department of Health (2010c) *Commissioning for Personalisation – A Framework for Local Authority Commissioners* [online] www.dhcarenetworks.org.uk.

Department of Health (2010d) *A Vision for Adult Social Care – Capable Communities and Active Citizens* [online] www.dh.gov.uk/publications.

Department of Health (2011) *Modernisation of Health and Social Care. Pathfinder Groups Bulletin* [online] www.dh.gov.uk/publications.

Department of Health (2012a) *White Paper – Caring for our Future – Reforming Care and Support* [online] https://www.gov.uk/government/organisations/department-of-health.

Department of Health (2012b) *NHS Future Forum Reports, First and Second Phase* [online] www.dh.gov.uk/publications.

Department of Health (2012c) *Health and Social Care Act 2012* [online] www.legislation.gov.uk.

Department for Works and Pensions (2008) *Commissioning Strategy* [online] www.dwp.gov.uk/cr-rep-08.pdf.

Field, R (2012) *Planning and Budgeting Skills for Health and Social Work Managers.* London: SAGE Publications.

Glasby, J (2012) *Commissioning for Health and Wellbeing – An Introduction.* Bristol: Policy Press.

Gordon, A and Probert P (2012) *Future Council, The Role of the Local Authority in a Changing Public Service Landscape* [online] www.essex.gov.uk.

In Control (2009) *A Framework for Commissioning: Model Guidance – A Resource for Local Authorities* [online] www.in-control.org.uk.

Institute for Government (2010) *The State of Commissioning – Preparing Whitehall for Outcomes Based Commissioning* [online] www.instituteforgovernment.org.uk.

InWent (2009) *Managing Collaboration, Management Model for Successful Collaboration in the Public Sector* [online] http://www.hrdp-net.in.

Ipsos MORI/BMA (2011) *Doctors Are Most Trusted Profession – Politicians Least Trusted* [online] www.ipsos-mori.com.

Mays, N (1997) *Total Purchasing: A Profile of National Pilot Projects.* London: King's Fund.

Ministry of Justice (2011) *Commissioning Support Guidance, An Introduction to NOMS Offender Services Commissioning* [online] www.justice.gov.uk/downloads/publication.

National Audit Office (2012a) *Getting Value for Money from Procurement – How Auditors Can Help* [online] www.nao.org.uk/guidance.

National Audit Office (2012b) *Healthcare Across the UK: A Comparison of the NHS in England, Scotland, Wales and Northern Ireland 2012.*

NHS Commissioning Board (2012) *Clinical Commissioning Group Authorisation, Draft Guide for Applicants* [online] www.commissioningboard.nhs.uk.

NHS Information Centre (2008) *Information for World Class Commissioning* [online] www.ic.nhs.uk/webfiles/commissioning.

ONS (2010a) *National Population Projections – 2010-Based Reference Volume*, Series PP2 Release [online] www.statistics.gov.uk.

ONS (2010b) *Pension Trends, Life Expectancy and Healthy Ageing*, June 2010 [online] www.statistics.gov.uk.

ONS (2012) *Population Ageing in the United Kingdom, Its Constituent Countries and the European Union* [online] www.statistics.gov.uk.

Personal Social Services Research Unit (2010) *The National Evaluation of Partnerships for Older People*, 2010 Projects [online] www.dh.gov.uk/en/Publicationsandstatistics/Publications/PublicationsPolicyAndGuidance/DH_111240.

Scally, G and Donaldson, L J (1998) Clinical governance and the drive for quality improvement in the new NHS in England. *British Medical Journal* (4 July), 61–65.

The Health Foundation (2004) *Primary Care-Led Commissioning*, October.

Thompson, J (1997) *Strategic Management – Awareness and Change.* London: International Thompson Publishing.

Timmins, N (2001) *The Five Giants, A Biography of the Welfare State.* Harper Collins.

97

Index

360-degree web-based stakeholder survey 42

access to health services 86–7
accountability 9, 92
acute years care 64
adaptation 25
adaptive improvement 25
adult social care: challenges of commissioning
69; developing view of 59–65; development
of commissioning 50–3; government
actions 53–9; local authority spending
52; provision to prevention/shift 53–6;
residential to community care/shift 53–6;
role of local authorities 66–8; sociological/
economic factors 51–3
adversarial behaviour, commissioner–provider
14, 48, 78
age groups, spending by 76
ageing population 51–2
ambulance trusts 28
Any Qualified Provider 35
Association of Chief Executives of Voluntary
Organisations (ACEVO) 9
Association of Directors of Social Care 54
Association of Directors of Social Services 52, 54
Audit Commission 4, 5, 11, 15
authorisation process, of CCGs 41–6, 78
authority, unequal 15
autonomy, and Foundation Trusts 31

behaviour, challenging old 77–8
benefits, from commissioning 6–8
Best Value 10, 12, 15
Big Society 58
Blair, Tony 13 see also Labour government
boundaries, shared health/county and unitary
authorities 32
British Medical Association (BMA) 28, 39
budget decentralisation/devolution 12
budgets see also financial challenges; funding;
overspends: CCGs 81; Community
Budgeting 10, 13; local government 81;
personal budgets 56, 57; pooled budgeting
12–13
business acumen: of GPs 47; of practice
managers 47–8 see also commercial
acumen
business cases 12
business excellence model 9
business process re-engineering 9
business/service planning 9
business units 12

Cameron, David 13, 58, 59 see also coalition
government
care: numbers of people needing 60; numbers
of people receiving 52; packages of care 61;
sources of 59–60; stages of 55
care packages 61, 63
Care Quality Commission 37, 79
Care Services Improvement Partnership 4, 14, 50
care/support: whole life view of 61–4; wider
definition of 64
*Caring for Our Future: Reforming Care and
Support* 56, 57, 59, 64, 66
Central Procurement Directorate 9
challenges, facing NHS/social care 72–82
charities, as care givers 60, 73
Chief Social Worker 71
children's services, strategic partnerships 32
Children's Trusts 13
Chronically Sick and Disabled Act 1971 54
citizen-level commissioning 50
Civitas 31
Clark, Greg 58
client involvement, adult social care 56–7
client role, local authorities 12
Clinical Commissioning Groups (CCGs):
authorisation process 41–6, 78; budgets
81; Council of Members 41; formation
of 39–47; GP commissioning 47–9; GP
members 40; and GP practices 1, 37; lay
representation 79; leadership 42, 44, 47,
74; multi-professional focus 43; need to
behave differently 77–8; and NHS England
70; Organisational Development Plan 78;
Pathfinder CCGs 39; reviews of 46; service
development 81; shadow CCGs 39–40; as
social enterprises 39
clinical focus, CCGs 43
Clinical Governance 78
clinical input, to commissioning 33 see also
GP-led commissioning
clinical quality 34
clinical villages 34
clinicians: influence of/PCTs 30; and leadership
73–4; leadership training 78; professional
training 79
coalition government 35, 53, 57 see also
Cameron, David
collaboration: challenge of 79–80; between
commissioners 81; government
encouragement to 57–9; importance of 58;
multi-agency 12–13; public service 1; and
successful commissioning 14–16, 74; term 15